BRITISH RAILWAYS STEAMING FROM 'A-Z'

Compiled by
PETER HANDS

DEFIANT PUBLICATIONS
190 Yoxall Road
Shirley, Solihull
West Midlands

Printed on behalf of Richard Netherwood Ltd., by Gorenjski tisk d.d., Slovenia

CURRENT STEAM PHOTOGRAPH ALBUMS AVAILABLE FROM DEFIANT PUBLICATIONS

VOLUME 14
A4 size - Hardback. 96 pages
-178 b/w photographs.
£14.95 + £1.50 postage.
ISBN 0 946857 40 7.

VOLUME 15
A4 size - Hardback. 96 pages
-178 b/w photographs.
£16.95 + £1.50 postage.
ISBN 0 946857 52 0.

A 'VALEDICTION'
A4 size - Hardback. 96 pages
-173 b/w photographs.
£19.95 + £1.50 postage.
ISBN 0 946857 64 4.

VOLUME 1
A4 size - Hardback. 96 pages
-177 b/w photographs.
£14.95 + £1.50 postage.
ISBN 0 946857 41 5.

A4 size - Hardback. 96 pages
-174 b/w photographs.
£18.95 + £1.50 postage.
ISBN 0 946857 60 1

A4 size - Hardback. 96 pages
-177 b/w photographs.
£19.95 + £1.50 postage.
ISBN 0 946857 62 8.

VOLUME 11
A4 size - Hardback. 96 pages
-176 b/w photographs.
£16.95 + £1.50 postage.
ISBN 0 946857 48 2.

VOLUME 12
A4 size - Hardback. 96 pages
-176 b/w photographs.
£16.95 + £1.50 postage.
ISBN 0 946857 49 0.

VOLUME 1
A4 size - Hardback. 96 pages
-177 b/w photographs.
£14.95 + £1.50 postage.
ISBN 0 946857 39 3.

VOLUME 1
A4 size - Hardback. 96 pages
-174 b/w photographs.
£14.95 + £1.50 postage.
ISBN 0 946857 42 3.

VOLUME 2
A4 size - Hardback. 96 pages
-177 b/w photographs.
£19.95 + £1.50 postage.
ISBN 0 946857 63 6.

VOLUME16
A4 size - Hardback. 96 pages
-178 b/w photographs.
£18.95 + £1.50 postage.
ISBN 0 946857 61 X

CURRENT STEAM PHOTOGRAPH ALBUMS AVAILABLE AND OTHER TITLES

VOLUME 4
A4 size - Hardback. 96 pages
-177 b/w photographs.
£15.95 + £1.50 postage.
ISBN 0 946857 46 6.

A4 size - Hardback. 96 pages
-177 b/w photographs.
£15.95 + £1.50 postage.
ISBN 0 946857 45 8.

VOLUME 4
A4 size - Hardback. 96 pages
-177 b/w photographs.
£15.95 + £1.50 postage.
ISBN 0 946857 47 4.

VOLUME 3
A4 size - Hardback. 96 pages
-177 b/w photographs.
£17.95 + £1.50 postage.
ISBN 0 946857 54 7.

A4 size - Hardback. 96 pages
-169 b/w photographs.
£16.95 + £1.50 postage.
ISBN 0 946857 51 2.

A4 size - Hardback. 96 pages
-179 b/w photographs.
£17.95 + £1.50 postage.
ISBN 0 946857 53 9.

A4 size - Hardback. 96 pages
-174 b/w photographs.
£17.95 + £1.50 postage.
ISBN 0 946857 55 5.

VOLUME 4
A4 size - Hardback. 96 pages
-183 b/w photographs.
£17.95 + £1.50 postage.
ISBN 0 946857 57 1.

'50th' ALBUM
A4 size - Hardback. 96 pages
-186 b/w photographs.
£16.95 + £1.50 postage.
ISBN 0 946857 50 4.

VOLUME 5
A4 size - Hardback. 96 pages.
- 177 b/w photographs.
£17.95 + £1.50 postage.
ISBN 0 946857 58X.

VOLUME 5
A4 size - Hardback. 96 pages.
- 177 b/w photographs.
£17.95 + £1.50 postage.
ISBN 0 946857 59 8.

COMEDY
269 pages. Cartoons.
£9.95 + £1.00 postage.
ISBN 0 946857 30 X.

ACKNOWLEDGEMENTS

Grateful thanks are extended to the following contributors of photographs not only for their use in this book but for their kind patience and long term loan of negatives/photographs whilst this book was beinq compiled.

T.R.AMOS TAMWORTH	P.BARBER TAMWORTH	P.A.BRIDGMAN HUCCLECOTE
W.G.BOYDEN BEXHILL	B.W.L.BROOKSBANK MORDEN	N.L.BROWNE ALDERSHOT
L.BROWNHILL PWLLHELI	R.BUTTERFIELD MIRFIELD	P.CANE HATFIELD
R.S.CARPENTER BIRMINGHAM	NOBBY CLARK **	KEN ELLIS SWINDON
CHRISTOPHER FIFIELD LONDON	TIM FAREBROTHER BOURTON	A.N.H.GLOVER BIRMINGHAM
B.K.B.GREEN WARRINGTON	R.HARRIS NEW MALDEN	PETER HAY HOVE
M.F.HIGSON THE SMOKEBOX	R.W.HINTON GLOUCESTER	F.HORNBY NORTH CHEAM
A.C.INGRAM WISBECH	R.G.B.JACKSON KEMPSTON	ALAN JONES BATH
D.K.JONES MOUNTAIN ASH	B.W.LESLIE BEACONSFIELD	T.LEWIS *
B.J.MILLER BARRY	A.F.NISBET BRACKLEY	R.PICTON WOLVERHAMPTON
N.E.PREEDY GLOUCESTER	J.SCHATZ LITTLETHORPE	K.L.SEAL ANDOVERSFORD
C.P.STACEY STONY STRATFORD	TERRY WARD NORTHAMPTON	KIT WINDLE LOWER BREDBURY
MIKE WOOD BIRMINGHAM	N.WOOD DERBY	J.WRAITHMELL MIRFIELD

* Courtesy of the Norman Preedy collection.
** Courtesy of Mark Meeks.

Front Cover - 'L' is for *'Local Passenger'* - The wooden-posted LBSCR signal which dominates this picture controls the exit from the up (northbound) steam platform at Horsted Keynes. On 10th June 1954 the 3.55pm Oxted to Brighton *'local passenger'* with LMS Class 4 2-6-41 No 42102 hauling an ex. SECR 'birdcage' set, common passenger accomodation on the Oxted line for many years. (Peter Hay)

ISBN 0 946857 64 4

FIRST PUBLISHED 1998

INTRODUCTION

BRITISH RAILWAYS STEAMING FROM 'A-Z' is the final album to be released by 'Defiant Publications' and the author hopes the reader will enjoy the contents of the same. Within the pages of the same no famous names will be found and with the exception of one print, the last, no photographs which have been published before have been included.

Over sixty 'BR Steaming' albums have been produced since 1983, covering the 1950's, 1960's, Freight, Titled Trains and many regional areas such as Scotland, Wales and the North-West etc., along with the different Regions of British Railways from 1948-1968.

The majority of the photographs used in this album have been contributed by readers of Peter Hands series of booklets entitled 'What Happened To Steam' & 'BR Steam Shed Allocations' (both are still available) and from readers of the earlier 'BR Steaming Through The Sixties' albums. In normal circumstances these may have been hidden from the public eye for ever.

BRITISH RAILWAYS STEAMING FROM 'A-Z' contains the work of almost forty photographers and the author would like to take this opportunity to thank all of the individuals who have contributed photographs over the years.

The author would like to give a personal 'thank you' to all of the customers who have taken the time and trouble to purchase 'Defiant Publications' books since their inception in 1980 and hope they have enjoyed the memories of when 'Steam was King'.

All good things come to an end and after publishing railway books for some eighteen years, often in the face of financial adversity and disinterest from the 'Big Boys', the author has decided to 'hang his typewriter up', completing the cycle of turning a hobby into a business back into a hobby again.

Quoting the last lines from the author's 1982 book 'CHASING STEAM ON SHED', the appropriate ending to this eighteen year journey comes in the words of a chart-topping song from 1968 - 'Those where the days my friend, we thought they'd never end...'

For information on back numbers of the 'What Happened To Steam', 'BR Steam Shed Allocations' and 'BR Steaming' albums, please contact:

Tel. No.
0121 745-8421

Peter Hands,
190 Yoxall Road,
Shirley, Solihull,
West Midlands 890 3RN

CONTENTS

1) Snowy conditions prevail at Peterborough as BR Class 4 4-6-0 No 75060, from 15C Leicester (Midland), approaches the North station with an up local passenger train in the winter of 1958. No 75060 had been at 15C since new in May 1957. It departed from there in September 1962, moving the short distance to 17A Derby. Further transfers later in life took it to 8R Walton on the Hill, 8L Aintree, 8A Edge Hill (Liverpool), 9F Heaton Mersey and 6C Croes Newydd. (A.C.Ingram)

2) More snow, this time near to Brockham Green, as 70C Guildford based SR U Class 2-6-0 No 31630 heads a cross-country passenger from Redhill to Reading through frozen wastes in January 1962. Most Southern Region trains sported white discs, but in this case No 31630 is carrying the more traditional lamps on its bufferbeam. The end was on the horizon for No 31630 with condemnation looming in November 1962, after which it was cut up at Eastleigh Works. (A.C.Ingram)

3) Ashpits were an important feature of steam depots and many a spotter fell foul of them during 'bunking' sessions, especially at night. The author heard of one incident where an enthusiast hid in one in a successful attempt to hide from the railway police, peering at his potential captors through the driving wheels of a locomotive which was dropping occasional sparks on him. In this photograph we espy three engines at 5B Crewe (South) in June 1967. (D.K.Jones)

4) Most of the discarded ash at 70A Nine Elms on 14th July 1952 appears to have been dumped on the ground rather than in the adjacent ashpits as locally based SR N15 *King Arthur* Class 4-6-0 No 30755 *The Red Knight* is prepared for its next duty. Equipped with a large diameter chimney, *The Red Knight* was withdrawn from 70D Basingstoke in May 1957 and scrapped the same month. The name, however, lived on, later being carried by BR Class 5 4-6-0 No 73110. (R.W.Hinton)

5) Unlike the set-up at Nine Elms in the previous photograph, all is clean and tidy by the ashpits at 64A St.Margarets (Edinburgh) on 20th June 1964. Simmering over one of the pits in the company of an LMS Class 5 4-6-0 is LNER A4 Class 4-6-2 No 60023 *Golden Eagle* which had been drafted to 64A from 52A Gateshead in November 1963. A few days after this picture was taken, No 60023 was transferred to 61B Aberdeen (Ferryhill) where it was to die four months later. (P.Cane)

6) Despite looking in fine external fettle, GWR 5400 Class 0-6-0PT No 5403, newly allocated to 82D Westbury from 82A Bristol (Bath Road), is only two months away from withdrawal when captured by the camera at Trowbridge with trailer W86W after arriving from either Chippenham or Devizes in June 1957. The ranks of the 5400 Class were decimated by condemnations during the late fifties and by January 1960 only nine examples were still active. (R.S.Carpenter)

7) Amongst the final auto-trains operated by British Railways was the service from Gloucester (Central) to the Stroud Valley, the preserve of 85B Horton Road's surviving GWR 1400 Class 0-4-2 Tanks like No 1453 seen here departing from Gloucester bound for Chalford on a bright 10th October 1964. One month on and the service was no more as was No 1453. Stored at the closed Barnwood shed until January 1965, No 1453 was scrapped at Cashmores, Great Bridge. (N.E.Preedy)

8) As is well known towards the end of steam on the various regions, locomotives became run-down and were neglected by the cleaning staff, but some, like the ones in these two photographs, were a lot worse than others, hence the apt description - *'bedgraggled'*. Once of 82A Bristol (Bath Road) and 84A Wolverhampton (Stafford Road), 2B Oxley based GWR Castle Class 4-6-0 No 5063 *Earl Baldwin* is noted in steam at 2D Banbury on 8th November 1964. (Terry Ward)

9) Its identifying numbers almost obliterated by the grime, SR K Class 2-6-0 No 32350, of 75E Three Bridges, nears Fratton with a rake of empty coaching stock from Portsmouth Harbour on 1st September 1962. All seventeen members of this class were withdrawn *en masse* in November and December 1962 and for months, and years in some cases, were dumped at various locations before being called in for scrapping. No 32350 was cut up at Eastleigh in February 1963. (R.Picton)

10) Unlike the versatility of diesel traction, steam locomotives had to rely heavily on being serviced at depots before and after any particular rostered turn and as a result spent much of their time *'between duties'*. Resident LMS Class 6P5F 'Crab' 2-6-0 No 42909 is noted in the yard at 67C Ayr on 17th May 1964. For many years a Dumfries steed, No 42909 had been posted to Ayr during the same month. It survived in revenue earning service until January 1966. (T.R.Amos)

11) The mainstay of mineral train haulage in the Kingdom of Fife were the LNER J37 and J38 Class 0-6-0's based at Dundee (Tay Bridge), Dunfermline and Thornton Junction sheds. The J37's, built by the North British Railway, were numerically superior and one of their ranks, No 64619, shows off its simple lines as it simmers in the yard at Tay Bridge (62B) on 26th August 1957. No 64619 remained on the books at 62B until withdrawn in December 1963. (N.L.Browne)

12) Included in the heading *'between duties'* are those engines awaiting their turn of banking or pilot work which is the case with a duet of SR R1 Class 0-6-0 Tanks, Nos 31047 and 31337, at Folkestone Junction in May 1959 a month prior to being drafted to a final home at 70A Nine Elms. Note the Southern Region modernisation notice in the background proclaiming the forthcoming construction of three new berths for 12-car electric trains. (R.Butterfield)

13) Today, little is left to remind us of this once timeless railway scene at Oswestry, on the borders of England and Wales, where, on 2nd September 1962, GWR *Manor* Class 4-6-0 No 7810 *Draycott Manor* awaits its next turn of duty along with GWR 5400 Class 0-6-0PT No 5410 at the local shed. The depot is long gone, as is the station, but a section of single track survives as does the former Cambrian Railways Works which is now sectioned into industrial units. (J.Schatz)

14) During these modern times of the motor car the *'boat train'* as we knew it is virtually a thing of the past. Back in the fifties it was only the landed gentry who could afford to sail the oceans of the world in cruise liners, but trains which gained access to the Channel Islands via steamers from Weymouth Docks were geared to travellers of more modest means. In this picture, taken in 1957, GWR 1366 Class 0-6-0PT No 1366 heads one such *'boat train'*. (R.S.Carpenter)

15) Its path cleared by a lower quadrant signal, SR Rebuilt *Merchant Navy* Class 4-6-2 No 35014 *Nederland Line* (70A Nine Elms) hurries through Basingstoke with the *'Bournemouth Belle'* in the summer of 1964. The origins of this train, complete with Pullman cars, goes back to the early 1930's (a Sunday's Only service). Such was its popularity it became a daily service in 1936, adopting the *Bournemouth Belle* title which remained steam hauled until 1966. (P.A.Bridgman)

16) *'Bufferstops'*, unsung and rarely noticed items, were invaluable in terms of safety and the south end of the open running shed at 63A Perth had an array of them, but by the end of 1962 their only purpose in life was to contain rows of condemned and lifeless engines. Nearest the camera are a pair of Pickersgill Caledonian Railway Class 3P 4-4-0's, one being No 54482 and LMS Class 3 2-6-2T No 40150, a once longstanding inmate of 60D Wick. (R.Butterfield)

17) *'Bufferstops'* came in all sorts of shapes and sizes and the one seen here in the far left of the frame is little more than a rectangular piece of wood affixed to a concrete loading stage. The scene is the small goods yard at Watton, on former Great Eastern Railway metals between Swaffham and Thetford (closed in 1964). Also present on this unknown date in 1957 is LNER J17 Class 0-6-0 No 65568 (31C Kings Lynn) which was withdrawn in September 1958. (R.S.Carpenter)

18) On the BR system there was an immense selection of *'coalers'* to be found. Many were constructed of wood and coal was supplied to engines via small tip-up wagons inside the structures - a dirty and thankless task. One such design could be found at 65B St.Rollox, closed in November 1966, situated in a rather grim part of Glasgow. Standing beneath the *'coaler'* in June 1963 is 61B Aberdeen (Ferryhill) based LNER A4 Class 4-6-2 No 60009 *Union of South Africa.* (R.W.Hinton)

19) Remaining in Scotland we move to the 'top-shed' at 64B Haymarket where we espy locally based LNER A2 Class 4-6-2 No 60530 *Sayajirao* standing near to a modern concrete *'coaler'* in the late fifties. After closure to steam in September 1963 the concrete structure was demolished by explosive charges, a remarkable feat considering the close proximity of running lines. *Sayajirao* spent most of its latter years based at 62B Dundee Tay Bridge. (R.S.Carpenter)

20) The concrete *'coaler'* at 70A Nine Elms was a grim-looking affair and one had to have a head for heights to clamber into the building atop the same. Rendered redundant after the closure of Nine Elms shed early in July 1967, this was one of the last active *'coalers'* in London. In the left of the frame on Saturday 18th March 1967 is locally based BR Class 3 2-6-2T No 82029 which also survived until the closure of 70A, being cut up in 1968 at Birds, Risca. (N.Wood)

21) Apart from the armed forces there were few vocations which evoked *'comradeship'* quite like the railways did back in the days of steam. Looking relaxed and smiling for the camera at 82E Bristol Barrow Road in 1964 in front of BR *Britannia* Class 4-6-2 No 70051 *Firth of Forth*, from 5A Crewe (North), are, from left to right - fireman Mark Meeks, driver Sam Summerhill and driver Sid King. Note the 'nicked' Gloucester (Eastgate) totem in the right of the frame. (Nobby Clark)

22) Locally based at 62B, BR Class 4 2-6-4T No 80123 blasts its way through the *'cutting'* at Tayport with the 7.11pm local passenger train to Dundee Tay Bridge on 6th July 1964. A longstanding occupant of the depot at Tay Bridge, No 80123 was transferred to a new (and final) home at 66A Polmadie (Glasgow) in March 1965. Condemned from the same in August 1966 it was stored at 66A for two months before making a last journey to Faslane for scrapping. (A.F.Nisbet)

23) Shortly after departing from Beaconsfield with the 12.20pm local from High Wycombe to Marylebone on 18th May 1958, LNER L1 Class 2-6-4T No 67747, from 34E Neasden, raises the echoes as it storms through the *'cutting'* near to the station as it heads towards London. In the last four years of active service, No 67747 was also allocated to 1A Willesden, 9G Gorton and 40E Colwick. Withdrawn from the latter in July 1962 it was cut up at Darlington. (B.W.Leslie)

24) Showing the value of smoke deflectors, begrimed BR *Britannia* Class 4-6-2 No 70049 *Solway Firth*, of 1A Willesden, leaves a trail of white smoke as it steams through *'Roade Cutting'* with an empty stock working on a gloomy 28th March 1964. Constructed by July 1954 and initially allocated to 6J Holyhead, No 70049 was not named until May 1959. It served from a host of sheds on the LMR before being condemned from 12A Carlisle (Kingmoor) in December 1967. (Terry Ward)

25) Things can be hardly more *'derelict'* than this evocative shot of Neasden shed, once coded 34E and 14D under BR, on 1st May 1966, almost four years after closure. The outside of the former Great Central Railway six-road structure looks more akin to a scene from the aftermath of a World War One battle than a once busy depot. Situated near to Wembley stadium it was not unusual for Neasden to host locomotives from five different regions at any one time. (C.P.Stacey)

26) For many years prior to closure in late 1967, the roofless roundhouses at Tyne Dock (54B and 52H) would at first glance give an impression the depot was *'derelict'*, but in fact they were utilised by 'live' steam engines almost until the end. Looking rather forlorn inside one of the roundhouses on a wet day in 1958 is former North Eastern Railway J25 Class 0-6-0 No 65675, which, surplus to requirements at 52A Gateshead, has been 'dumped' at Tyne Dock. (R.S.Carpenter)

27) Whilst steam locomotives were stored there was always an outside chance one or two might be steamed again, but once they reached their final destination, a scrapyard, they were *'doomed'*, with the unique exception of Barry Docks. On 8th April 1968 the 'cutters torch' is at work on the almost complete remains of BR Class 4 4-6-0 No 75052 (withdrawn from 5D Stoke in August 1967) at Birds, Long Marston. Soon, No 75052 will become a distant memory. (Mike Wood)

28) Although still sporting its numberplate, former Lancashire and Yorkshire Railway Class 2P 2-4-2T No 50725 is *'doomed'* at Looms of Spondon in the early summer of 1959 in the company of sister engine No 50646. Withdrawn from 55G Huddersfield in October 1958, No 50725 was stored along with many other loco types at Badnalls Wharf, Norton Bridge for many months prior to being ignominiously dragged to Looms where it was cut up during 1959. (M.F.Higson)

29) No *'A-Z'* picture album would be complete without including the once common sight of *'double-headers'*. With a clear road ahead, LMS Class 5 4-6-0's Nos 45105 (26A Newton Heath) and 45305, of 5B Crewe (South), hurtle past some parked lorries at Farnley Junction at the head of a lengthy express consisting of 'blood and custard' coaches on a sun-filled 16th June 1957. No 45105 was condemned in October 1966, but No 45305 is still with us today. (B.K.B.Green)

30) Working bunker-first, LMS Class 2 2-6-2T No 41305 and SR W Class 2-6-4T No 31916, both of 71A Eastleigh, combine their resources to power a heavy train of oil tanks in wooded countryside at New Pooks Green on the Fawley branch on 28th July 1961. No 31916 took its leave of Eastleigh shed in November 1962, moving to 72A Exmouth Junction, followed by No 41305 in September 1963, which was drafted to Wemouth. Both were withdrawn by June 1965. (D.K.Jones)

31) Maximum effort on Dainton bank as 83C Exeter St.Davids based GWR *Grange* Class 4-6-0 No 6820 *Kingstone Grange* pilots an unidentified GWR *Castle* Class 4-6-0 past the diminutive signalbox and sidings with an express in the summer of 1953. In later years *Kingstone Grange* went on to work from the sheds at 85A Worcester, 86G Pontypool Road, 86A Newport (Ebbw Junction) and 88A Cardiff East Dock. Condemned in July 1965, No 6820 was cut up at Birds, Morriston. (R.S.Carpenter)

32) Under partially clear signals, SR M7 Class 0-4-4T No 30104, from 71B Bournemouth and BR Class 3 2-6-2T No 82016, of 71A Eastleigh, provide excess power for a three-coach passenger train seen here departing from Millbrook for Southampton on 5th December 1959. Records show us that No 30104 was withdrawn from 71B in May 1961 whereas No 82016 was transferred to 70C Guildford in December 1962. It survived in revenue earning service until April 1965. (T.R.Amos)

33) The *'engine and brake'* is virtually extinct today, with the exception of preserved railways, but in steam days they were a common sight as they set off on their daily routine to pick up wagons from the host of small goods yards which many individual stations possessed. Possibly fresh from overhaul at Wolverhampton Works 83B Taunton based GWR 7400 Class 0-6-0PT No 7436 trundles towards Wednesbury tunnel in the heart of the Midlands on 30th December 1959. (T.R.Amos)

34) Travelling tender-first with its brakevan, locally based (81D) GWR *Modified Hall* Class 4-6-0 No 7904 *Fountains Hall* is noted at Reading on 21st September 1964. For many years an 81A Old Oak Common steed, No 7904 had a stint at 81D from December 1963 until April 1964 when it returned to 81A. One month later and it was back at 81D, this time until December 1964, moving to 85A Worcester. Its last abode was at 81F Oxford, being withdrawn in December 1965. (D.K.Jones)

35) The final photograph in this brief sequence of *'engine and brake'* shots is of another locally based mount in a tender-first position. With a member of the footplate crew looking forwards from his charge, LNER B1 Class 4-6-0 No 61176 (51C) clatters along at West Hartlepool on 13th September 1963. Once of 51A Darlington, No 61176 was allocated to 51C from June to December 1963. Its final allocations were at 50B Hull (Dairycoates) and 50A York. (D.K.Jones)

36) With its new coat of paint glistening, GWR *Modified Hall* Class 4-6-0 No 7914 *Lleweni Hall*, from 81D Reading, stands silently by the turntable at Swindon Works after overhaul on 12th August 1962 in the company of condemned GWR 5700 Class 0-6-0PT No 7764, withdrawn from 88C Barry in May of the same year. Remaining at 81D until April 1964, *Fountains Hall* then had a flurry of transfers to 82B St.Philip's Marsh, 82E Bristol Barrow Road and 81F Oxford. (N.L.Browne)

37) A quartet of locomotives stand proudly in the yard at Crewe Works after emerging from the paint shop in September 1962. By a quirk of fate all four engines are from depots on other regions. From left to right they are as follows:- LMS Class 8F 2-8-0 No 48346 (41E Staveley Barrow Hill), LMS Class 5 4-6-0 No 44853 (55A Leeds - Holbeck), BR *Britannia* Class 4-6-2 No 70037 *Hereward the Wake* (40B Immingham) and BR Class 9F 2-10-0 No 92044 (36A Doncaster). (L.Brownhill)

38) *'Ex.Works'* from Eastleigh, SR U1 Class 2-6-0 No 31893 stands proudly alongside the running shed at 70B Feltham on 17th December 1959 which had been 'home' to this engine after a move from 73E Faversham in June of the same year. After a spell at 73J Tonbridge, from June 1960 until May 1961, No 31893 was drafted to 75E Three Bridges. The U1's, twenty-one in total, were intact as a class at the end of 1961, but twelve months on only four examples survived. (N.E.Preedy)

39) Many 'foreign' types were outshopped from Cowlairs Works, including the LNER J39 Class 0-6-0's, one of which, No 64987 (54C Borough Gardens), gleams in bright sunshine in the yard at 65A Eastfield (Glasgow) in August 1952. Behind No 64897 is LNER V4 Class 2-6-2 No 61700 *Bantam Cock* and in the right of the frame is LNER A4 Class 4-6-2 No 60004 *William Whitelaw.* No 64897 returned to Cowlairs Works for scrapping after withdrawal in December 1962. (R.W.Hinton)

40) *'Fast Freight'* came in a number of guises, from partially fitted to fully fitted vacuum-braked trains, including livestock, fruit, milk and perishables. On 18th April 1964, 81D Reading based GWR *Grange* Class 4-6-0 No 6863 *Dolhywel Grange* is obviously working hard as it approaches Wednesbury tunnel with a fully fitted freight at speed as it heads towards Birmingham. During the following month No 6863 was drafted to a final home at 88A Cardiff East Dock. (T.R.Amos)

41) LMS Class 5 4-6-0 No 44776, from 21A Saltley, passes a wooded area near to Westerleigh with a fitted freight consisting of a mixture of wagons on 5th July 1961. In October 1962, No 44776 was reallocated to 17A Derby, but returned to Saltley in July of the following year after a brief stint at 15C Leicester (Midland). It later served from the sheds at 2A Tyseley, 6C Croes Newydd and 8F Springs Branch Wigan before being condemned in October 1967. (D.K.Jones)

42) 'Super-power' at the head of a down express freight as LNER A1 Class 4-6-2 No 60158 *Aberdonian*, of 34A Kings Cross, threads its way through Peterborough (North) under clear signals on 16th August 1958. To the right of *Aberdonian*, halted by signals, is an LNER 02 Class 2-8-0 on a freight and a diesel multiple unit. In the left of the frame is a cramped, but quite extensive goods yard and in the distance we can just make out the Crescent road bridge. (B.W.L.Brooksbank)

43) In the main footplate crews were indeed *'friendly'* (with the exceptions of those which used to cover up the cabside numbers as they passed through Tamworth (High Level) thwarting the efforts of the spotters in the field below near to the Low Level station to identify their steeds). On an unknown date in the fifties the young fireman of former Great Eastern Railway J15 Class 0-6-0 No 65475 (31A Cambridge) poses for the camera at Mildenhall. (R.S.Carpenter)

44) Both fireman and driver, complete with standard issue British Railways caps (still seen today on preserved lines) smile towards the camera from the cab of their charge, LMS Class 8F 2-8-0 No 48154, from 2B Nuneaton, as it trundles past the photographer at Stockport in June 1961. Ousted from Nuneaton in August 1962, No 48154 experienced a flurry of transfers up until withdrawal in July 1967, including 1E Bletchley, 6C Birkenhead and 10F Rose Grove. (R.W.Hinton)

45) Also sporting standard headgear, this *'friendly footplate crew'* have adopted a similar stance to members of a 'tiger hunt' who have just returned with their 'prize' and want their photograph recorded for posterity! As they are doing so, their charge, 85E Gloucester (Barnwood) based Class 0F 0-4-0T No 41535 is becoming impatient as it awaits its next shunting movement at Sudbury in Gloucester in 1958. No 41535 survived in service until October 1964. (R.W.Hinton)

46) With his fireman looking a little self-conscious, the driver of SR Unrebuilt *Merchant Navy* Class 4-6-2 No 35021 *New Zealand Line* (71B Bournemouth) appears to have chosen to pose as a 'Hollywood Hardman' as he casually leans out of his cab window at London's Waterloo station in 1958. Note the differing styles of headgear. *New Zealand Line*, rebuilt at Eastleigh Works in June 1959, remained at Bournemouth shed until rendered redundant in August 1965. (D.K.Jones)

47) Proceeding under caution BR *Clan* Class 4-6-2 No 72009 *Clan Stewart*, from 12A Carlisle (Kingmoor), draws into Stirling with a Euston to Perth express (1S53) on 2nd August 1964. Allocated to Kingmoor from new in March 1952, this final member of the *Clans* had a brief flirtation at 30A Stratford between September and October 1958 before fleeing home again a month later. Some examples of the class had a distinctive red background on their nameplates. (N.E.Preedy)

48) The pioneer member of the *Clans*, No 72000 *Clan Buchanan*, although somewhat grubby, is the subject of admiration at Carlisle (Citadel) station on a misty day in April 1958 shortly after being reallocated to 66A Polmadie (Glasgow) from 64B Haymarket, where it had been since October 1957. Shedded at 66A Polmadie after being released into traffic in December 1951, *Clan Buchanan*, in common with Nos 72001-4, was withdrawn in December 1962. (D.K.Jones)

49) Locally based at Kingmoor shed, No 72007 *Clan Mackintosh* opens its cylinder cocks in the yard of the same during the summer of 1965, its last year of service. By the end of 1965 there were only two surviving members of these rather unpopular and shortlived Pacifics, Nos 72006 *Clan Mackenzie* and 72008 *Clan Macleod*, both allocated to 12A. A few months later and the class disappeared into history with the withdrawal of No 72006 in May 1966. (D.K.Jones)

50) Possibly recognised as one of the most famous named trains in the world, steam carried the flag for the *Golden Arrow* on this side of the channel until 11th June 1961, being hauled for the last time by SR Rebuilt *West Country* Class 4-6-2 No 34100 *Appledore*. On 15th June 1958, SR Unrebuilt *West Country* Class 4-6-2 No 34092 *City of Wells*, of 73A Stewarts Lane, approaches Headcorn with *'The Arrow'*. Happily, *City of Wells* is still with us today. (Peter Hay)

51) Nearing the end of steam haulage, the *Golden Arrow* passes through Ashford with the down working on 5th April 1961 powered by SR Rebuilt *West Country* Class 4-6-2 No 34101 *Hartland*, also from Stewarts Lane shed. Serving later from the depots at Bricklayers Arms, Brighton, Nine Elms and Eastleigh, *Hartland* (withdrawn in July 1966) was salvaged from Barry for preservation in July 1978 by enthusiasts of the Peak Railway in Derbyshire. (Christopher Fifield)

52) The term *'Greyhound'* was applied to the SR T9 Class 4-4-0's because of their free-running abilities. Designed by Dugald Drummond, once the Locomotive Superintendent of the North British and Caledonian Railways before joining the London and South Western Railway, all of the T9's were paired with ungainly eight-wheeled tenders because the LSWR had no water troughs. At rest in the shed yard at 70F Fratton on 6th October 1956 is No 30732, a local steed. (F.Hornby)

53) An immaculate-looking *'Greyhound'*, No 30288, another local engine (71A), takes a breather at the apparently deserted station at Eastleigh on 18th May 1955 whilst in charge of a three-coach 'blood and custard' local passenger from Didcot. The *'Greyhounds'* were to fall early victim to modernisation and all but one, No 30120 (later preserved), were withdrawn by July 1961. No 30288 was taken out of traffic from 71A in December 1960 and cut up at the nearby works. (N.L.Browne)

54) Looking in fine external fettle two former Great Eastern Railway locomotives are seen *'head to head'* in the cramped shed yard at 32D Yarmouth (South Town) - circa 1955. Nearest the camera is LNER F4 Class 2-4-2T No 67162 whose origins go back as far as 1884. Facing No 67162 is LNER D16 Class 3P1F 'Claud Hamilton' 4-4-0 No 62544, a local resident of 32D. Both engines were withdrawn in the fifties with No 62544 the last to go in December 1959. (R.S.Carpenter)

55) Another *'head to head'*, this time at Bournemouth station on 9th July 1964. Facing a BR Standard type is SR Rebuilt *West Country* Class 4-6-2 No 34032 *Camelford*, from 70E Salisbury. For many a long year *Camelford* was allocated to 72A Exmouth Junction before moving to Salisbury in October 1963. Constructed in June 1946, No 34032 was rebuilt at Eastleigh Works in October 1960. Condemned from 70E in October 1966 it was scrapped at Buttigiegs, Newport in 1967. (Alan Jones)

56) Situated in the heart of the *'Highlands'*, Aviemore is a thriving ski centre today and also the main base for the Strathspey steam centre. Back in the early sixties it was just an anonymous town on the railway map which was in the transition of changing from steam to diesel power. 'On shed' at 60B on 4th July 1961 are two LMS Class 5 4-6-0's, one of which can be identified as No 45453 (63A Perth), and an English Electric Type 1 Diesel. (D.K.Jones)

57) No 62274 *Benachie* was the last of the D40 Class 4-4-0's to enter service as Great North of Scotland Railway Class 'F' in 1921. She was one of eight superheated locomotives built by the North British Locomotive Company in Glasgow and at Inverurie Works, all bearing names of local significence. *Benachie* is seen fully coaled in front of the running shed at 61C Keith on 29th June 1955. One example of the class, *Gordon Highlander*, is preserved. (R.Butterfield)

58) As *'inclines'* go the 'Lickey Incline' takes some beating with its fearsome gradient of 1 in 37 from Bromsgrove to the summit at Blackwell. On a sunny day in August 1961, LMS Class 5 4-6-0 No 44767, from 55A Leeds (Holbeck) and fitted with Caprotti valve gear, heads a Bristol to Leeds express (M994). It would appear from the exhaust fumes that the banker seems to be doing more than its share of the work. No 44757 moved to 8M Southport in November 1963. (N.E.Preedy)

59) Many *'inclines'*, by nature of the terrain, were situated in remote places, but few were more remote than those on the now long-closed Cromford and High Peak Railway - Cromford - Sheep Pasture - Middleton Top. To gain access to the latter one had to consult an Ordnance Survey Map. It was situated about one and a half miles north of Wirksworth and half a mile south of Middleton village and on 25th August 1952, LMS Class 2F 0-6-0T No 58850 is noted there. (B.J.Miller)

60) In the West Country one the most notorious *'inclines'* was Dainton bank in Devon, between Aller Junction and the summit at Dainton tunnel and varies between 1 in 46 and 1 in 36 (summit) for two and a half miles, a daunting task for the strongest of engines. With some spotters in the frame and a clear road ahead, GWR *Castle* Class 4-6-0 No 5071 *Spitfire* (83A Newton Abbot) attacks Dainton with the heavily loaded down *Cornishman* on 26th July 1955. (R.W.Hinton)

61) *'Inspection Saloons'* were exclusively the preserve of the railway hierarchy and employees used to shudder and shrink into the shadows when news of their imminent arrival was passed along the 'grapevine'. One such saloon (no doubt with its own 'hospitality-cupboard' on board) is noted near to Tamworth (High Level) station with LMS Class 2 2-6-0 No 46522 (2F Bescot) in charge on 25th August 1965. Within less than two years No 46522 was a memory. (P.Barber)

62) The *'Irish Mail'* came into being on 18th June 1849 with its first departure from Euston carrying mails bound for Ireland. On a summer's day in 1961, LMS *Princess* Class 4-6-2 No 46207 *Princess Arthur of Connaught*, from 1B Camden, is in its eleventh hour as it powers the *Irish Mail* at Crewe. Once of 8A Edge Hill (Liverpool), No 46207 was to serve twice from Camden and Willesden sheds in London before being taken out of service in November 1961. (Kit Windle)

63) During the early sixties when steam was being slaughtered on the mainland the *'Isle of Wight'* was a mecca for spotters and photographers alike with its unique combination of ancient carriages and 100% steam haulage by the SR 02 Class 0-4-4 Tanks based at 70H Ryde. On a bright 7th July 1963, No 27 *Merstone* runs round the stock of the 1.30pm passenger from Ryde Pier Head at an almost deserted Cowes station which was destined to close at the end of 1966. (J.Schatz)

64) A trio of well dressed ladies stand back as No 28 *Ashey* steams into Ryde St.Johns with the 1.33pm to Cowes on 15th July 1962. The rail system in the *'Isle of Wight'* was decimated during the fifties and the 'Beeching Axe' in 1966 almost completed the job. The only route open today is from Ryde Pier Head to Sandown utilising former London Underground trains. Steam lives on from Haven Street on the closed route to Cowes using the preserved No 24 *Calbourne*. (R.Picton)

65) The *'Jubilee'* Class 4-6-0's were extremely popular engines and were to be found on all regions with the exception of the Southern throughout their thirty-three years of service. On 3rd February 1955, No 45646 *Napier*, from 25G Farnley Junction, steams beneath an impressive signal gantry as it arrives at Manchester (Victoria) with an express. *Napier* remained at Farnley Junction until condemned in December 1963. Scrapping took place at Darlington Works. (B.K.B.Green)

66) With a station clock informing us it is twenty minutes or so after ten o'clock in the morning, No 45717 *Dauntless*, of 27A Bank Hall (Liverpool), is unusually employed on the 3.00am express from Leeds (City) at Bristol (Temple Meads) on 6th August 1963. Three months on and *Dauntless* was no longer with us, its ultimate fate being decided by the cutter's torch at Cowlairs Works in February 1964. The *'Jubilees'* were rendered extinct as a class in November 1967. (J.Schatz)

67) *'Junctions'* come in all sizes and this is a rather impressive example at Heaton Norris where LMS Class 5 'Caprotti' 4-6-0 No 44744 (22A Bristol Barrow Road) steams by with an express on a sun-filled 21st May 1956. No 44744 moved on to pastures new at 17A Derby in May 1957, serving later from 27A Bank Hall, 27C Southport and 9A Longsight (Manchester). Of the 842 members of the class, No 44744, along with No 45485 were the only ones the author never saw. (T.Lewis)

68) Barmouth Junction in deepest Wales was one of the smallest *'junctions'* on BR and ceased being the same when the line to Dolgelly and Bala closed during 1965, being renamed 'Morfa Mawddach'. On an unknown date in the fifties, BR Class 2 2-6-0 No 78007, from 89C Machynlleth, is noted at Barmouth Junction with a freight working. This locomotive ended its days on the LMR, at 5A Crewe (North), 5B Crewe (South), 9G Gorton, 9E Trafford Park and 9K Bolton. (R.S.Carpenter)

69) The LNER inspired *'K1'* Class 2-6-0's, designed by Peppercorn, were constructed from 1949 under BR and numbered a total of 70 units. With youth on their side they avoided the mass withdrawals of 1962, but the inevitable occurred during 1963 when 10 were condemned. All were gone by September 1967 with the exception of No 62005 which was retained for steam heating duties at the ICI plant at Port Clarence. No 62039 is pictured at Wisbech during the fifties. (R.S.Carpenter)

70) The Gresley Great Northern *'K2'* 2-6-0's were first introduced in 1914 and modifications were carried out on some from 1931. Many were based in Scotland for use over the West Highland line, such as No 61791 *Loch Laggan*, seen here in the company of other engines in the yard of its home shed at 65J Fort William on 26th June 1959. The Scottish examples were all gone by August 1961, with *Loch Laggan* being condemned in March 1960 and scrapped at Connells, Calder. (A.N.H.Glover)

71) Of the K Class engines the *'K3'* 2-6-0's were by far the most numerous with different variations amongst their ranks. They were shedded at depots on the Eastern, North Eastern and Scottish Regions being employed in the main on freight and passenger services. Newly transferred to 40E Colwick from 31B March, No 61861 is a 'guest' outside the running shed at 41H Staveley GC on 16th December 1960. It was withdrawn from 34E New England in January 1962. (D.K.Jones)

72) The five engines from the *'K4'* Class 2-6-0's, Nos 61993 *Loch Long*, 61994 *The Great Marquess*, 61995 *Cameron of Lochiel*, 61996 *Lord of the Isles* and 61998 *Macleod of Macleod* were introduced in 1937 for service on the West Highland line. Pictured here in steam in the yard of its home shed, 65A Eastfield (Glasgow), is No 61995 on 6th November 1955. All were condemned from 62A Thornton Junction in October 1961 with No 61994 being earmarked for preservation. (R.Butterfield)

73) The mighty *'King'* Class 4-6-0's, with their tractive effort of 40,285lbs, were the most powerful locomotives on the Western Region and for many years they dominated the crack expresses on the routes from Paddington to Plymouth and from Paddington to Wolverhampton. Once of 83D Laira (Plymouth), No 6027 *King Richard I*, from 84A Wolverhampton (Stafford Road), climbs up the gradient from Hockley and arrives at Birmingham (Snow Hill) with an up express in 1961. (R.S.Carpenter)

74) Destined to be the last active member of the *'Kings'*, No 6018 *King Henry VI*, of 81A Old Oak Common, pauses at Newbury station with an express in 1958. Transferred to 86C Cardiff (Canton) in August 1961, No 6018 returned to Old Oak Common in June 1962. Although officially withdrawn in December 1962 it was retained at 84E Tyseley for an SLS special to Swindon on 28th April 1963 to and from Birmingham (Snow Hill) via the Greenford loop and Oxford. (R.S.Carpenter)

75) Of the variants of the British Railways *'Lion-on-Wheel'* logos the larger example, as seen adorning the tender of former Great Eastern Railway D16 Class 'Claud Hamilton' 4-4-0 No 62548, probably stood out more than the others. No 62548, from 31B March, is noted with a fully laden tender at Ely station on a down passenger train in the mid-fifties. Condemned from March shed in September 1957, No 62548 was cut up at Stratford Works two months later. (R.S.Carpenter)

76) LNER B1 Class 4-6-0 No 61247 *Lord Burghley*, allocation not known, sports the large *'Lion-on-Wheel'* on its straight-sided tender as it departs under clear signals from March station (Joint Great Eastern/Great Northern) with a passenger working during the fifties. Note the brazier alongside the water column in the foreground. *Lord Burghley* later worked from the depots at 36A Doncaster and 40E Colwick before being withdrawn in June 1962. (R.S.Carpenter)

77) As an enthusiast there is nothing better, especially in quiet reflectful moments, than the sound of *'leaking steam'* from live locomotives. The next four prints are dedicated to this simple man-made feature. On a bright 16th May 1954, locally based former North British Railway D34 Class 'Glen' 4-4-0 No 62487 *Glen Arklet* simmers in front of the vast running shed at 64A St.Margarets (Edinburgh). For *Glen Arklet* its steaming days came to an end in September 1959. (F.Hornby)

78) Purloined by the shed staff at either Oxley or Stafford Road sheds following repairs at Wolverhampton Works, steam escapes from 81C Southall based GWR 6100 Class 2-6-2T No 6156 as it shunts coaching stock at the Low Level station on 25th March 1959. Before being condemned in December 1965, No 6156 was also allocated to the depots at 81E Didcot (twice), 81F Oxford (twice) and 81A Old Oak Common in addition to two further spells at Southall. (T.R.Amos)

79) Shrouded in steam, February 1945 constructed SR Rebuilt *Merchant Navy* Class 4-6-2 No 35013 *Blue Funnel*, a local inhabitant of the near-at-hand shed (70F), prepares to depart from Bournemouth (Central) with a Weymouth to Waterloo express on 23rd August 1966. For many years a favourite at 72A Exmouth Junction, *Blue Funnel* was drafted to Bournemouth in September 1964. Its final abode was at 70A Nine Elms, being withdrawn in July 1967. (Alan Jones)

80) Steam drifts lazily from the near vicinity of the smokebox of former Caledonian Railway Class 3P 'Dunalastair IV' 4-4-0 No 54446 (withdrawn before the end of the fifties), which is sporting the stencilled lettering of its relatively new owner at Carstairs shed on 9th June 1949. Also *'leaking steam'* in the background is LMS Class 4 2-6-4T No 42173 with a 'star' on its smokebox door. Carstairs was coded 28C, 64D and 66E and closed in December 1966. (A.N.H.Glover)

81) *'Light Engines'* are still part of the railway scene today and as they pass by the average onlooker, few, apart from those who rostered them and the footplate crews manning them, know from whence they came or where they are going! In this close-up, LNER A2/1 Class 4-6-2 No 60508 *Duke of Rothsay* (35A New England) is one such beast at Grantham station in 1953. Of the earlier A2's, Nos 60501-10, all were destined for early retirement from service by July 1961. (R.S.Carpenter)

82) Looking in pristine condition, Wainwright inspired SR C Class 0-6-0 No 31723, of 70C Guildford, is noted *'light engine'* at Clapham on a sunny 7th July 1956. The C Class 0-6-0's were the largest of their type in service on the Southern in numbers, but by January 1962 they had been whittled down to just twenty-one working examples. All were withdrawn by June 1962 with the exceptions of Nos 31271/80 and 31592 which were transferred to Departmental Stock. (N.L.Browne)

83) At every locomotive depot there was a *'line-up'* of engines, especially on Sundays, and spotters would eagerly scuttle from one to the other recording the numbers. On 7th August 1965, LMS Class 0F 0-4-0T No 41528 is hemmed between a trio of Riddles War Department Class 8F 2-8-0's out in the open at 41E Staveley Barrow Hill. No 41528 was 'officially' drafted to 41J Langwith Junction in October 1965, but this was nothing more than a paper transfer. (C.P.Stacey)

84) A dismal day outside the running shed at 34E New England on 1st September 1963 where a *'line-up'* of locos includes two LMS Class 4 'Flying Pig' 2-6-0's and LNER A4 Class 4-6-0 No 60007 *Sir Nigel Gresley*, a resident of 34E since the closure of 34A Kings Cross in June of this same year. In October 1963, No 60007 was on the move again, this time to a new lease of life in Scotland where it spent much of its remaining time on the Glasgow-Aberdeen services. (K.L.Seal)

85) The *'local passenger'* is still a key element of the railways today, but there is very little to match steam hauled ones in terms of variety, just the same old boring diesel or electric multiple units. On 14th April 1961, SR U Class 2-6-0 No 31626, of 71A Eastleigh, sets off from Southampton (Central) with such a working. Once a servant of 72A Exmouth Junction and 72C Yeovil, No 31626 had been at 71A since February 1960. It was withdrawn in January 1964. (T.R.Amos)

86) Another *'local passenger'* is noted in bright sunshine at Nottingham (Victoria) - circa 1957. In charge of the local at this former Great Central Railway station is Gresley designed LNER J39 Class 0-6-0 No 64976 which has had its cabside number 'bulled-up' by the footplate crew from 38A Colwick. In January 1957 there were 289 members of this class, but all were gone by December 1962. No 64976 was condemned from Colwick shed in November 1959. (R.S.Carpenter)

87) For spotters the *'loose-coupled'* goods trains were as much a part of their everyday lives as the steam locomotives which hauled them, but were way down the pecking order compared to the illustrious express workings. With a member of the footplate crew staring into space, locally based (56C) LNER J6 Class 0-6-0 No 64277 rattles by the camera at Copley Hill, Leeds with a freight in May 1961. No 64277 was one of the last J6 survivors, going in June 1962. (D.K.Jones)

88) LMS Class 4F 0-6-0 No 44583, from 21A Saltley, is noted near to the locomotive depot at New England, Peterborough with a down *'loose-coupled'* goods in December 1958. When 'rationalisation' was introduced during the infamous Beeching era it spelt the death knell for these trains and thousands of wagons were consigned to the scrap metal merchants. Today, *'loose-coupled'* goods trains are as much a rarity as are the brakevans which once accompanied them. (A.C.Ingram)

89) With apologies to GWR and LNER fans, lack of space has restricted the heading of *'majestic'* to just two prints. The author hopes they will capture the spirit of the halcyon days of steam in all its glory, unfettered by overhead wires and growling diesels. On 15th September 1954, locally based LMS *Royal Scot* Class 4-6-0 No 46161 *King's Own* (9A Longsight) departs from Manchester (London Road) with the up *Mancunian* bound for London (Euston). (B.K.B.Green)

90) SR Unrebuilt *Merchant Navy* Class 4-6-2 No 35003 *Royal Mail*, of 72A Exmouth Junction, sweeps majestically through Clapham with the 3.00pm express from Waterloo to the West of England on 6th July 1957. Built at the height of the Second World War in September 1941, *Royal Mail* was rebuilt in August 1959. Serving later from the depots at 70A Nine Elms (twice), 70F Bournemouth and 70G Weymouth, No 35003 was withdrawn from the latter in early July 1967. (N.L.Browne)

91) Larger locomotives were placed on *'menial duties'* for a variety of reasons, but as steam power was usurped by diesel locomotion there were simply no other tasks to put the survivors on. Such is the case with uncared-for GWR *Castle* Class 4-6-0 No 7022 *Hereford Castle*, from 85B Gloucester (Horton Road), which has been seconded by the shed staff at 2A Tyseley to power a local passenger at Birmingham (Snow Hill) on a miserable day in March 1965. (D.K.Jones)

92) When steam was in its prime, larger engines were often employed on *'menial duties'* as running-in turns after visits to workshops. This may well be the reason why LNER A3 Class 4-6-2 No 60039 *Sandwich* (35B Grantham) is in charge of another local turn at Great Ponton at the foot of Stoke bank during the mid-fifties. Introduced into service in 1934, *Sandwich* acquired a double chimney during July 1959 and German style smoke deflectors in June 1961. (R.S.Carpenter)

93) To spotters the lure of *'motive power depots'* was beyond temptation and hence the expression 'bunking' became part of railway vocabulary. On 'official' visits with a shed pass one could strut around like a 'Cock o' the North', which is presumably why the photographer is out in the open at 65J Fort William on 26th March 1955. A small number of locomotives are to be seen in steam, including LMS Class 5 4-6-0 No 45011, complete with snowplough. (B.K.B.Green)

94) Much of the trackwork within the vicinity of the depot at 70B Feltham has been lifted on 8th November 1964 and judging by the empty roads within the running shed its resident population has been depleted by withdrawals. Standing in the shed yard is a BR Class 9F 2-10-0 and a SR S15 Class 4-6-0. In the left of the frame, dwarfed by the coaling plant, are three other locomotive types. Closing to steam in July 1967, its remaining steam stock went for scrap. (C.P.Stacey)

95) Steam *'motive power depots'* came in all shapes and sizes, from vast, multiple roundhouses to this small stone-built structure at Kyle of Lochalsh, a sub-shed of 60A Inverness. Inside the two-road structure is an LMS Class 5 4-6-0 and alongside the building, in steam, is former Caledonian Railway Class 2P 0-4-4T No 55216 (60A) on 18th May 1954, which was condemned in October 1961 and scrapped at Inverurie Works in early 1962. (F.Hornby)

96) 24B Rose Grove on 10th September 1961 where we can espy several locomotives in steam, including LMS Class 4 2-6-4T No 42298, a visitor from 24C Lostock Hall. Generally speaking railwaymen were a friendly lot, but when on 'bunking' sessions one had to be wary of angry foremen and irate shedmasters and during these 'unofficial' visits spotters tended to act like escaped 'prisoners of war', lurking in the shadows with their notebooks. (R.S.Carpenter)

97) LNER B1 Class 4-6-0 No 61323, from 31B March, is well '*off-the-beaten-track*' as it attacks the stiff climb towards and through Monument Lane tunnel whilst departing from Birmingham (New Street) with the empty stock of the 1.42pm passenger from Peterborough on 14th April 1960. By this stage in time, with the mass introductions of diesel multiple units and locomotives, it was extremely rare to observe steam engines from March at New Street. (B.W.L.Brooksbank)

98) Looking completely out of place, SR U Class 2-6-0 No 31807, of 75C Norwood Junction, is also '*off-the-beaten-track*' being sidelined between the roundhouse and longshed at 1A Willesden on 'Cup Final' day in May 1963. Note the lack of BR emblem on the tender of No 31807. Once of 70F Fratton, 70C Guildford and 75B Redhill, No 31807 had been at Norwood Junction since December 1962. It was condemned from the same in January 1964 and cut up at Eastleigh. (R.G.B.Jackson)

99) One *'odd-ball'* was the LNER Gresley 4-cylinder compound high pressure locomotive, W1 Class 4-6-4 No 10000, nicknamed the 'Hush-Hush' engine, which first appeared in 1929. During 1937 it was rebuilt with 3-cylinders and was similar in appearance to the LNER A4 Class 4-6-2's, with its 'wedge-front', streamlining and valances. The latter was removed under the Thompson regime and 10000 became No 60700 under BR. It is seen here at Kings Cross in June 1952. (Peter Hay)

100) Another *'odd-ball'* adorned the infamous scrapyard at Darlington for many years. Although withdrawn from 51F West Auckland in January 1958, the remains of LNER Y1 Class 0-4-0T No 68149 were still in use as a store as late as 1963. Darlington Scrapyard was a sad and dismal place to visit and amongst the more illustrious locomotive types cut up here were LNER A3 Class 4-6-2's Nos 60082, 60086, 60088, 60100, 60108 and BR *Clan* Class 4-6-2's No 72000-4. (D.K.Jones)

101) Many railway photographs, either by accident or design, became *'panoramic'*, this being the case at Gloucester on 20th June 1957, as LMS Class 5 4-6-0 No 45056, of 19B Millhouses, passes Horton Road shed (85B) and steams into Eastgate station with a lengthy passenger working from the Birmingham direction. Prior to withdrawal in August 1967, No 45056 worked from a number of different depots, including Holyhead, Rugby, Nuneaton and Speke Junction. (D.K.Jones)

102) *'Parcels'* trains were a common sight all over the British Railways system during the days of steam and many types of engines were employed to haul them. On a dull late summer's day in early September 1963, LMS *Coronation* Class 4-6-2 No 46240 *City of Coventry* clatters over pointwork at Chester (General) with a *'parcels'* from Holyhead. For many years a great favourite at 1B Camden, *City of Coventry* had been transferred to 1A Willesden the previous month. (Kit Windle)

103) Before freight services were centralised in vast marshalling yards, the *'pick-up'* was an essential part of railway life, especially in rural areas before the advent of the road 'juggernauts' as we know today came into being. Most of these trains were hauled by 0-6-0 types, like former Midland Railway Class 2F No 58168 (21A Saltley) seen approaching Rubery in 1955 with a Halesowen to Longbridge working. Rubery had closed to passengers in 1927. (R.S.Carpenter)

104) Due to shortages of suitable motive power, especially during hectic summer services, many underpowered locomotives were *'pressed into service'* on trains normally rostered for more powerful types. Under the watchful gaze of two youths, GWR 4300 Class 2-6-0 No 5333, from 84E Tyseley, is at Birmingham (Snow Hill) with a express during the fifties. With the introduction of diesels the ranks of the 5300 series was decimated from 1958 onwards. (R.S.Carpenter)

105) *'Quadrupled'* was the most common driving wheel arrangement for the haulage of heavy freight trains and a close look at the tractive effort of the locomotives in the next three frames make rather interesting comparisions. In this first photograph, GWR Churchward 2800 Class 2-8-0 No 2850 (35,380lbs t.e.), of 84B Oxley, nears the camera with a heavy goods train bound for South Wales at Grange Court Junction on the outskirts of Gloucester in 1956. (N.E.Preedy)

106) Travelling tender-first on the High Dyke (freight only) branch, work-stained LNER Gresley 02 Class 2-8-0 No 63931 (36,740lbs t.e.), from 34F Grantham, provides the motive power for a rake of iron-ore empties in 1962. Of a total of sixty-six engines, some forty examples were still at work by the end of 1962, but by October 1963 all were withdrawn. No 63931, condemned from 36A Doncaster in September 1963, was scrapped during the following month. (D.K.Jones)

107) Almost at the end of steam on BR, LMS Stanier Class 8F 2-8-0 No 48348 (32,440lbs t.e.), with chalked numerals and shedcode on the smokebox door, has been 'spruced-up' in readiness for enthusiasts specials in the yard of its home shed at 10F Rose Grove on a sunny Wednesday 31st July 1968. From January 1957 onwards, No 48348 was allocated to 8B Warrington, 6C Birkenhead (twice) and 6B Mold Junction before going on the books at Rose Grove in June 1965. (N.Wood)

108) With a former Caledonian Railway 0-4-4T in the background, ex. North British Railway J37 Class 0-6-0 No 64536 (64C Dalry Road) is fully coaled and *'ready for work'* in the shed yard at 63A Perth on 18th June 1949. Note that someone has made a half-hearted attempt to obliterate the LNER initials on the tender of No 64536. Reallocated to 64A St.Margarets (Edinburgh) in September 1958, No 64536's career was brought to an end in May 1959. (W.G.Boyden)

109) Hands behind his back a railwayman studies something on locally based BR *Britannia* Class 4-6-2 No 70014 *Iron Duke* which is more than *'ready for work'* on its next duty, the *Night Ferry*, at 73A Stewarts Lane on 29th September 1951. Originally allocated to 32A Norwich from new in June 1951, No 70014 was drafted to 70A Nine Elms during the same month, moving to 73A three months later. It left the Southern for good in June 1958, going to 14B Kentish Town. (R.S.Carpenter)

110) Although all of the regions utilised *'reporting numbers'*, it was the Western Region which really made them stand out, as can be seen in the next two prints. GWR *Castle* Class 4-6-0 No 4090 *Dorchester Castle* (F41), of 87A Neath and with white painted buffers, takes the East loop at Gloucester with a Paddington to Swansea express in early 1962. *Dorchester Castle* had been diverted via Gloucester due to engineering work in the Severn tunnel. (P.A.Bridgman)

111) Not long released from the Testing Plant at Rugby, 86C Cardiff (Canton) based BR *Britannia* Class 4-6-2 No 70025 *Western Star* powers *The Red Dragon* (720) near to Reading in August 1953. Both *The Red Dragon* and *The Capitals United* expresses were the preserve of the Canton *Britannias* until they were transferred to the London Midland Region in 1961. *Western Star* was initially drafted to 21D Aston along with sister engines Nos 70017, 70024, 70026-29. (D.K.Jones)

112) From the late fifties onwards the simple word *'redundant'* took on a sinister meaning when countless railwaymen lost their jobs as the 'rush to modernise' took its toll on machines and men. This process was speeded up with the appointment of Doctor Beeching. Rendered *'redundant'* from 1E Bletchley in December 1962, former LNWR Class 7F 0-8-0 No 49078 rotted in a siding at Nuneaton shed until around October 1964 before being scrapped at Looms, Spondon. (Terry Ward)

113) Bereft of coupling rods, a trio of *'redundant'* former Pickersgill Caledonian Class 3P 4-4-0's, Nos 54474, 54483 and 54475, present a sorry sight as they stand cold and lifeless in a 'dead' road at 65B St.Rollox on a misty 15th June 1958. Although not 'officially' withdrawn for many months to come it is extremely doubtful if any of them were steamed again. Although not condemned until June 1961, No 54483 had been in store since April 1950. (F.Hornby)

114) In direct contrast to the forlorn locomotives on the previous page, SR Rebuilt *Merchant Navy* Class 4-6-2 No 35028 *Clan Line* has been *'restored'* to its former glory and is seen on show at the now long closed Longmoor Military Railway during an 'Open Day' on 28th September 1968. *Clan Line*, constructed in December 1948 and rebuilt in October 1959, went straight into preservation after withdrawal from 70A Nine Elms in July 1967, courtesy of the MNLPS. (F.Hornby)

115) Earmarked for preservation many years beforehand, former Great Eastern Railway N7/4 Class 0-6-2T No 69621 seeks a safe haven inside 55H Leeds (Neville Hill) in August 1964 in the company of LNER K4 Class 2-6-0 No 3442 (61994) *The Great Marquess*. Many, many years were to pass by before both of these steam engines were actively *'restored'*. No 69621 was withdrawn from 30A Stratford when the depot closed its doors to steam in September 1962. (J.Wraithmell)

116) The *'sacked chimney'* was often the 'mark of doom' for steam engines and as more and more were laid off on a temporary or permanent basis the more this particular feature was seen at motive power depots. Pickersgill Caledonian Class 3P 4-4-0 No 54489, although fully coaled, has suffered the indignity of the *'sacked chimney'* syndrome at 63A Perth on 26th August 1957. However, No 54489 was later resurrected and lived on until December 1961. (N.L.Browne)

117) Designed by Holmes and of North British Railway origin, LNER J83 Class 0-6-0T No 68456 is laid up in a rusting siding at 62A Thornton Junction with a *'sacked chimney'* on 21st June 1959. Two months later and No 68456 was given a new lease of life by being transferred to 64E Polmont, situated between Edinburgh and Glasgow. Time was not on the side of No 68456 and it was withdrawn from Polmont in January 1961. It was scrapped later at Inverurie Works. (A.N.H.Glover)

118) The *'Sandringham'* B17 Class 4-6-0's designed by Gresley were introduced in 1928 because of the need for higher powered engines on the G.E. main line. A total of seventy-three were built and most were named after famous houses and football clubs. From 1945 ten examples were rebuilt by Thompson, creating the B2 Class. No 61664 *Liverpool*, from 32D Yarmouth South Town and withdrawn in June 1960, is seen in the shed yard at 31A Cambridge during the fifties. (R.S.Carpenter)

119) During 1937 the Great Eastern authorities streamlined two of the *'Sandringham'* B17's in the same manner as the A4's and they were utilised on the *East Anglian* express from Liverpool Street to Norwich. One of the B2 examples, BR No 61671 *Royal Sovereign*, was maintained as the Royal Engine up until withdrawal in September 1958. Also seen in the yard at 31A Cambridge in the fifties, No 61626 *Brancepeth Castle* is a visitor to the shed from 31B March. (R.S.Carpenter)

120) The '*Schools*' Class locomotives were destined to be the most powerful 4-4-0's in Europe and were amongst the most handsome engines ever designed. Officially designated as 'V' Class engines they were able to operate on all of the Southern main lines and regularly worked trains of 350 tons on tight schedules. During the fifties, No 30917 *Ardingly*, from 74B Ramsgate and fitted with a large diameter Lemaitre multiple jet blastpipe, is noted at 75A Brighton. (Tim Farebrother)

121) Two '*Schools*' similarly equipped with the same blastpipe arrangement are prepared for their next duties in the yard at 74C Dover (Priory) on 13th August 1957. Nearest the camera is No 30918 *Hurstpierpoint* (74B Ramsgate) and behind the same is No 30930 *Radley* (73B Bricklayers Arms). Ousted from the Kent Coast route by third rail electrification in 1960/61, most spent the remainder of their lives at depots like Brighton, Basingstoke and Nine Elms. (N.E.Preedy)

122) The *'self-weighing'* tender was little used by British Railways steam locomotives and their exact purpose in life is somewhat of a mystery to the author. If some kind person could enlighten him he would be grateful. On 23rd August 1964, LMS Class 5 4-6-0 No 44697 is paired with one in the yard of its home shed at 9D Newton Heath. A longstanding inmate at Newton Heath, No 44697 was taken out of service from the same during November 1967. (T.R.Amos)

123) Surplus to requirements, former Caledonian Railway Class 2P 0-4-4 Tanks, Nos 55169, 55173 and 55217 are *'sidelined'* alongside the running depot at Arbroath, a sub-shed of 62B Dundee Tay Bridge, on 30th June 1955. At some later time the fortunes of all three changed for the better and they worked from the depots at 66A Polmadie (Glasgow), 60B Aviemore and 62A Thornton Junction respectively. No 55217 was the last to be withdrawn, in August 1962. (R.Butterfield)

124) Without *'shed pilots'* the daily activities of the larger steam depots would have been heavily hampered. Rostered for this tedious duty at 22B Gloucester (Barnwood) on 1st August 1953 is locally based ex. Midland Railway 2F Class 0-6-0 No 58206 which is shunting empty coaching stock. Condemned from Barnwood in July 1957, No 58206 was scrapped at Derby Works the same month. Barnwood shed, also coded 85E and 85C, closed completely on 10th May 1964. (R.W.Hinton)

125) As in the above print, many *'shed pilots'* came from the ranks of 'work-worn' classes eking out their final days before being taken out of service. On 18th September 1954, McIntosh Caledonian Class 3P 4-4-0 No 54439, built in 1907 and rebuilt eight years later, shunts loaded wagons up the hump to the coaling stage at 68B Dumfries. No 54439, one of only two members of this particular class, was withdrawn well before the fifties came to a close. (R.Butterfield)

126) A carriage window reflects the trail of white exhaust steam as 9B Stockport based BR *Britannia* Class 4-6-2 No 70015 *Apollo* tackles the *'single line'* stretch of track out of Dundee and heads for Perth with an express in August 1965. No 70015 also worked from the sheds at Camden, Stratford, Old Oak Common, Cardiff (Canton), Trafford Park, Newton Heath, Neasden, Annesley, Willesden, Llandudno Junction, Crewe (South) and Carlisle (Kingmoor). (Kit Windle)

127) With a long-winded warning notice of the penalties of trespass in the foreground, unkempt-looking BR Class 4 2-6-4T No 80081, from 70F Bournemouth, rattles along on single track at Lyncombe Vale with a three-coach local passenger train on 24th April 1964. No 80081, allocated to 1E Bletchley from new in March 1954 and to 1A Willesden in November 1959, was transferred to the Southern Region during the same month. It was withdrawn from 70F in June 1965. (R.Picton)

128) Despite working hard as it comes up the gradient, LMS Class 5 4-6-0 No 44693 (56F Low Moor) has *'steam to spare'* as it powers the Bradford bound *Yorkshire Pullman* at Laisterdyke on 3rd May 1967. One of a numerical trio of three such engines allocated to Low Moor for many years (44693-95) all were transferred to 56D Mirfield in April 1964, but by November 1966 they were reunited at 56F. No 44693 was withdrawn shortly after this picture was taken. (N.E.Preedy)

129) Once of 17D Rowsley, locally based LMS Class 4F 0-6-0 No 44250 lifts its safety valves as it passes the weed-strewn and soon to be closed station at Heaton Mersey during the summer of 1960 with a lengthy goods train. No 44250 remained on the books at Heaton Mersey until February 1964, moving to 16E Kirkby. Following withdrawal from the latter in May 1965, No 44250 was stored for a couple of months before being scrapped at Wards, Beighton. (R.W.Hinton)

130) GWR *Castle* Class 4-6-0 No 4000 *North Star*, of 84A Wolverhampton (Stafford Road) has *'steam to spare'* whilst in charge of an express at Exeter St.Davids on 1st September 1952. *North Star* originally appeared as 'Atlantic' 4-4-2 No 40 in 1906. It was rebuilt as a *Star* Class 4-6-0 in 1909 becoming No 4000 and finally, in 1929, it became a *Castle* Class 4-6-0. *North Star* was condemned from 87E Landore in May 1957 after completing 2,110,396 miles. (A.N.H.Glover)

131) *'Stovepipes'* did little to enhance the looks of steam engines and were applied in the main to locomotives of Caledonian Railway origin. On 6th November 1955, LMS Class 2P 0-4-4T No 55237 is seen in the yard of its home shed at 66A Polmadie (Glasgow) in the company of an LMS Class 6P5F 'Crab' 2-6-0 and LMS *Coronation* Class 4-6-2 No 46231 *Duchess of Atholl.* No 55237, withdrawn in July 1961, was cut up at the C & W Works, Heatheryknowe, Glasgow. (R.Butterfield)

132) Drummond Caledonian Class 2F 0-6-0 No 57345 shows off its *'stovepipe'* chimney whilst on parade at 63A Perth on 26th August 1957. This picture clearly shows the spartan protection to adverse weather conditions afforded to footplate crews on some of the more elderly types of locomotives. No 57345, on the books at Perth shed for many years, succumbed to the inevitable in February 1962 and after a period of storage at Forfar shed was scrapped. (N.L.Browne)

133) Towards the end of steam many a proud locomotive was *'stripped of nameplates'* either for safekeeping or by being stolen by over-zealous spotters. Such is the case with SR Rebuilt *Battle of Britain* Class 4-6-2 No 34089 *602 Squadron*, from 70E Salisbury, which has paused at Southampton (Central) on an August day in 1966 with the 11.30am from Waterloo to Bournemouth. Once of 73A Stewarts Lane and 75A Brighton, No 34089 was withdrawn in July 1967. (Ken Ellis)

134) With its tender 'looking' ex.works, GWR *Grange* Class 4-6-0 No 6815 *Frilford Grange* (86E Severn Tunnel Junction) has been *'stripped of nameplates'* as it assembles a train of oil tanks at Southall on 20th September 1965. An 83B Taunton engine for many years, No 6815 was transferred to 83D Laira (Plymouth) in June 1961. From August 1962 until August 1965 it was allocated to 87F Llanelly and 88A Cardiff East Dock. Condemnation came in November 1965 from 81F Oxford. (D.K.Jones)

135) By the very nature of the surroundings and the locomotives themselves many railway photographs produced a combination of '*sunlight and shadow*'. This picture is a perfect example as the sun highlights GWR 5600 Class 0-6-2T No 6601 and 82D Westbury based 5700 Class 0-6-0PT No 8744 in steam near to the coaling stage at 82B St.Philip's Marsh during 1960. No 6601 departed from 82B in January 1962, finding a new home at 88H Tondu in the Welsh Valleys. (D.K.Jones)

136) With the sun almost at its zenith unusual shadows are cast inside one of the roundhouses at 14A Cricklewood during the fifties. The main focus of attention is LMS Class 3F 0-6-0T No 47200, which was built by the Vulcan Foundry in 1899 and fitted with condensing apparatus. Both No 47200 and attendant sister engine, No 47209, were taken out of service from Cricklewood shed in April 1961. The former was scrapped at Gorton and the latter at Derby. (R.S.Carpenter)

137) There is deep shadow in the near vicinity of Basingstoke station as the sun beats off SR N Class 2-6-0 No 31408, from 70C Guildford, as it powers the 8.45am semi-fast passenger from Woking on 25th August 1964. No 31408 had a varied selection of homes during its life, including 73A Stewarts Lane, 73F Ashford and 72B Salisbury. Allocated to 70C in August 1963 it remained in service there until taken out of revenue earning service in June 1966. (D.K.Jones)

138) Shadow almost obliterates the front end of work-stained BR Class 4 2-6-4T No 80041, of 73F Ashford, as it rounds a curve and steams into Maidstone East station with a local working bound for its home town on 3rd March 1961. Released into traffic in July 1952, No 80041 was allocated to 1E Bletchley. It moved to the Southern Region at Ashford shed in November 1959 and ended its days at 83G Templecombe, being withdrawn from the same in March 1966. (B.W.L.Brooksbank)

139) BR Class 9F 2-10-0 No 92212, from 2A Tyseley and equipped with a double chimney, passes Gloucester South Junction signalbox as it eases a Bristol bound freight out of a siding on 30th January 1966. Although steam had officially ended in the Gloucester and Bristol areas at the end of 1965 there were occasional forays by the same utilising engines from the London Midland Region. Today, No 92212 is actively preserved at the Great Central Railway. (N.E.Preedy)

140) Also equipped with a double chimney, BR Class 9F 2-10-0 No 92248, of 82E Bristol Barrow Road, heads a freight train towards Mangotsfield at Staple Hill, Bristol on 23rd August 1963. No 92248 (withdrawn in May 1965) had a brief lifespan of less than five and a half years during which it also worked from the depots at 86A Newport (Ebbw Junction) and 21A Saltley before being transferred from Barrow Road to 88A Cardiff East Dock in January 1965. (T.R.Amos)

141) The Eastern Region employed a host of BR Class 9F 2-10-0's at a cross-section of motive power depots until steam was eradicated from the same in June 1966. With the station pilot in the frame, locally based (35A New England) No 92036 heads a freight through Peterborough (North) in 1957. Transferred to 36A Doncaster in September 1962, No 92036 later had two stints at 40E Colwick and two further ones at New England prior to withdrawal in December 1964. (R.S.Carpenter)

142) Like the *'self-weighing'* tenders, locomotives with *'tender-cabs'* were very much a rarity, but compared to the 'open-plan' footplate of the engine in caption No 132, the protection afforded to former Caledonian Railway Class 2F 0-6-0 No 57472 is bordering on the 'luxurious'. No 57472, in good external condition, is pictured in the yard of its home depot at 65D Dawsholm on 4th June 1949. It was destined to die at the same in September 1961. (A.N.H.Glover)

143) The *'Terriers'*, or rather the SR A1X Class 0-6-0 Tanks, were extremely popular little engines, both with footplate crews and enthusiasts alike and were famous for their duties on the Hayling Island branch up until its closure during 1963. No 32650 is pictured at Eastleigh shed on 10th November 1963, a depot it been home to since moving from 70F Fratton in November 1959. Shortly after withdrawal, No 32650 was preserved at the Kent and East Sussex Railway. (N.L.Browne)

144) For onlookers on stations the sight of *'through traffic'* stimulated their senses as trains hurtled towards them one minute and were gone the next, often accompanied by a shrieking whistle. On 7th June 1965, LMS Class 5 4-6-0 No 44794, from 61B Aberdeen (Ferryhill), passes Alyth Junction station (closed in 1967) with the 4.07pm mail train from Aberdeen. Four months before Ferryhill shed closed to steam in March 1967, No 44794 was posted to 63A Perth. (K.L.Seal)

145) LMS *Royal Scot* Class 4-6-0 No 46114 *Coldstream Guardsman*, of 9A Longsight (Manchester), presents a fine sight as it storms past Cheadle Hulme station with the up *Comet* from Manchester (London Road) to Euston on 8th September 1953. Transferred at a later date in the fifties to 8A Edge Hill (Liverpool), No 46114 was also based at the sheds at Willesden (twice), Bushbury, Llandudno Junction, Holyhead and Annesley before withdrawal in September 1963. (B.K.B.Green)

146) The *'tunnel'* is still an important feature of the modern railway scene of today (though not quite the same unless filled with smoke). To trainspotters they were necessary evils and frustrating places to travel through. On 22nd July 1961, BR Class 4 2-6-0 No 76027 (71A Eastleigh) emerges from the *'tunnel'* outside Southampton (Central) with a passenger working. Built by October 1953, No 76027 remained a 71A steed until March 1962, moving to 71B Bournemouth. (T.R.Amos)

147) Once an everyday scene at steam motive power depots, the essential *'turntable'* has all but disappeared today and most are to be found at preserved sites like the Didcot Railway Centre and at Kidderminster on the Severn Valley Railway. On 5th July 1953, SR Unrebuilt *Battle of Britain* Class 4-6-2 No 34073 249 *Squadron* is turned at Dover. Surplus to requirements on the Kent Coast route due to electrification, No 34073 moved to 70A Nine Elms in May 1961. (B.K.B.Green)

148) Looking fresh from overhaul at Doncaster Works, LNER A4 Class 4-6-2 No 60028 *Walter K. Whigham*, of 34A Kings Cross, is rotated at 31A Cambridge during the fifties. Constructed in 1937 as No 4487 this locomotive was originally named *Sea Eagle* (a name carried later by LNER A1 Class 4-6-2 No 60139). It was amongst the first members of the class to be withdrawn from 34A in December 1962, the others being Nos 60003, 60014, 60030 and 60033. (R.S.Carpenter)

149) The squat, cut-down chimney as affixed to former North British Railway J36 Class 0-6-0 No 65285, seen in the yard of its home shed at 65E Kipps on 3rd July 1955, has turned a handsome locomotive into an *'ugly'* one. Kipps shed, situated near to Coatbridge (Sunnyside) station, closed to steam in January 1963 with the bulk of its remaining stock going for scrap. No 65285 had made its escape from the depot in December 1962, moving to 65B St.Rollox. (R.Butterfield)

150) The LMS Caprotti Class 5 4-6-0's are a 'must' when considering candidates to come under the classification of *'ugly'*. On 24th March 1951, No 44756, of 20A Leeds (Holbeck), passes Hellifield with an express. The 'Caprotti's', Nos 44738-44757, although having youth on their side (built during 1948), were obviously not considered a success as all were withdrawn between April 1963 and January 1966. No 44756 was condemned in September 1964. (B.K.B.Green)

151) In the author's humble opinion the SR Q1 Class 0-6-0's, which looked like a cross between a 'meccano' toy and a 'prehistoric creature', came top of the heap in the *'ugly'* stakes. This 'basic' of 'basic' designs came about because of the need for a powerful locomotive which could run over the whole system during the Second World War - thus 'looks' were sacrificed to save weight. No 33008 is seen 'at home' at 70B Feltham on 26th May 1963. (T.R.Amos)

152) This situation at Swindon comes under the category of the *'unusual'* where locally based GWR 5700 Class 0-6-0PT No 9720 has had a slight 'altercation' with a new 120 Class diesel multiple unit as to 'what' was going 'where' in the summer of 1960. No 9720 was on a trip working to the near-at-hand 'Factory' from which a party of interested onlookers have emerged. The engine was was recovered by the breakdown crane and lived on until November 1961. (Ken Ellis)

153) Described as the 'engines which won the war', the LNER V2 Class 2-6-2's were first introduced by Gresley in 1936. They eventually numbered a total of 184 and some examples were modified with double chimneys and outside steampipes. In this 1960 picture, No 60819, from 64A St.Margarets (Edinburgh), displays its handsome lines in the yard at 64B Haymarket. From August 1962 until September 1963, No 60819 was part of the 'dump' at 64F Bathgate. (N.E.Preedy)

154) The Eastern Region owned a large number of the '*V2*' Class and they were allocated to depots like this one at 36A Doncaster where one of its inmates is captured by the camera in the shed yard on 8th September 1963 shortly before withdrawal. Nos 60831 (50A York) and 60836 (62B Dundee Tay Bridge) were the last to be condemned, in December 1966. The pioneer locomotive, No 60800 *Green Arrow* (named after an express freight service of 1936) is preserved. (K.L.Seal)

155) The *'V1'* Class 2-6-2 Tanks were another Gresley design and first came into service during 1930 with a 3MT rating. A modified version of the same (V3) was introduced in 1939 (4MT). Looking resplendent in a fresh coat of paint, No 67608 poses for the camera in the yard at 65A Eastfield (Glasgow) in 1961. By January 1963 modernisation had taken its toll and all of the Scottish based examples were gone. No 67608 was condemned from 65A in December 1962. (R.S.Carpenter)

156) *'Viaducts'* vary from the humble single-span versions to the mighty, like this extremely impressive one at Holmes Chapel which is being traversed by LMS *Royal Scot* Class 4-6-0 No 46126 *Royal Army Service Corps* which is in charge of an express on 8th August 1954. Most viaducts outlived the steam locomotives which once graced them, like No 46126, which passed into history after being withdrawn from 16D Annesley in October 1963 after which it was cut up at Crewe. (B.K.B.Green)

157) The humble and taken-for-granted *'water column'* went largely unnoticed during the days of steam, being just another 'common' feature of the railway environment. Parked near to one in the shed yard at 66A Polmadie (Glasgow) on 15th June 1958 is resident former Caledonian Railway Class 2F 0-6-0 No 57319, near to which is sister engine, No 57389. The former engine originally appeared as a '709' Class in 1890 and steamed for over seventy years before withdrawal. (F.Hornby)

158) Hands in pockets a railwayman appears disinterested as he stands on an embankment near the coaling stage at 9F Heaton Mersey on Saturday 2nd March 1968. Beneath him water gushes out of a *'water column'* and overflows from the tender top of LMS Class 8F 2-8-0 No 48344. This locomotive, newly transferred to Heaton Mersey from 9E Trafford Park shortly before the closure of the latter, was taken out of traffic a month after this picture was taken. (N.Wood)

159) With an impressive semaphore signal gantry in the frame and a gaggle of spotters on the platform, SR Unrebuilt *Battle of Britain* Class 4-6-2 No 34064 *Fighter Command* (70A Nine Elms) takes refreshment from a *'water column'* which has an extended arm at Southampton (Central) station on 5th August 1963. *Fighter Command*, equipped with a Giesl Oblong Ejector in May 1962, is in charge of the heavily loaded 8.35am express from Waterloo to Weymouth. (A.F.Nisbet)

160) With the station *'water column'* on guard at Ledbury in May 1963, GWR *Grange* Class 4-6-0 No 6856 *Stowe Grange* awaits the 'right away' before setting off for home at Worcester with the Hereford portion of a Paddington express. The abolition and removal of the once vast numbers of *'water columns'* from most of the former BR system has caused a lot of problems for steam specials over the years and today there is talk of reinstating some at key places. (Ray Harris)

161) This vast *'water tank'* stands atop the coaling facility at 8D Widnes, of London & North Western Railway origin, where, some sixteen months after nationalisation, LMS Class 2 2-6-0 No 46421 shows off its newly acquired BR number and stencilled lettering of its latest owner on 24th April 1949. After the complete closure of Widnes shed on 13th April 1964 this structure may well have disappeared into the dust of history with the crack of a gelignite charge. (B.K.B.Green)

162) The *'wooden-tender'* was a throwback to Victorian times and it is amazing that some examples managed to soldier on until the early nineteen sixties. With an ex. CR Class 2F 0-6-0 in the background, former CR Class 0F 'Pug' 0-4-0ST No 56029 is coupled to its 'tender' in the small shed yard at 65D Dawsholm in April 1958. This particular breed of locomotives, vintage 1885, became extinct in December 1962 with the withdrawal of No 56029 from 65E Kipps. (R.W.Hinton)

163) Every region of British Railways had at least one major *'workshop'* and they were generally 'off limits' to all but the most foolhardy of spotters unless one had a permit or was on an official visit. Most were vast and complex places and took some time to trek around on foot. On the Southern Region the main one was at Eastleigh, where, on 11th August 1960, SR Unrebuilt *West Country* Class 4-6-2 No 34105 *Swanage* (71B Bournemouth) is being overhauled. (P.Cane)

164) *'The'* most famous *'workshop'* on the Western Region was without doubt located at Swindon, birthplace of the mighty *Castles* and *Kings* in Great Western Railway days. In this 'birds-eye' view taken on 14th April 1949 a large variety of GWR steam engines in various states of repair are to be seen. These include: - *Hall* Class 4-6-0's Nos 4915 *Condover Hall* and 5979 *Cruckton Hall*, 4300 Class 2-6-0 No 6393 and *Saint* Class 4-6-0 No 2981 *Ivanhoe*. (D.K.Jones)

165) The *'Xtra'* was a bonus for spotters and often had a surprise package as the motive power as is possibly the case with this special which has 56B Ardsley based LNER A3 Class 4-6-2 No 60080 *Dick Turpin* at its head in the summer of 1962 near to the site of Cotehill station (closed in 1952) on the Settle & Carlisle. Equipped with a double chimney in October 1959 and German style smoke deflectors in November 1961, No 60080 was withdrawn in October 1964. (R.S.Carpenter)

166) Sweeping past an unusual set of 'double' semaphores, LMS *Coronation* Class 4-6-2 No 46239 *City of Chester* (1B Camden) speeds southwards through Bletchley with an *'Xtra'* from Blackpool to Euston on 24th May 1958. At this stage in time there were fourteen of these fine locomotives based at Camden, the others being Nos 46229, 46236, 46237, 46240, 46241, 46242, 46244, 46245, 46247, 46250, 46254, 46256 and 46257. All were gone from 1B by September 1963. (B.W.L.Brooksbank)

167) *'York'* was a mecca for steam enthusiasts and the meeting place for locomotives not only from the North Eastern Region, but from the Eastern, London Midland and Scottish Regions. Not only was there a constant stream of expresses to be seen, but freight traffic also played a major part in the overall railway scene. LMS Class 5 4-6-0 No 44667, from 10J Lancaster (Green Ayre), passes Holgate station with a lengthy rake of empty flats on 25th June 1964. (B.W.L.Brooksbank)

168) Such was the busy state of affairs at *'York'* several station pilots were employed at any one time, mostly of the 'small engine' type like LNER J71 Class 0-6-0T No 68240 which is noted on such a duty at the south end of the station in the mid-fifties. During the early sixties, another 'small engine', LNER J72 Class 0-6-0T No 68736 was employed as a station pilot at York in North Eastern Railway colours, as was sister engine No 68723 at Newcastle. (R.S.Carpenter)

169) As disembarked passengers mill around on the station platform, GWR 6100 Class 2-6-2T No 6128, from 81B Slough, sports express headlamps and the special reporting number *'Z11'* at Marlow on 21st April 1963. Once of Southall and Kidderminster sheds, No 6128 had been at Slough since March 1962. Between May 1964 and withdrawal in March 1965 it rotated between 85B Gloucester (Horton Road) and Southall, being condemned from the former depot. (J.Schatz)

170) The running of two Ian Allan inspired specials on 4th March 1967 marked the ending of through trains between Paddington and Birkenhead. GWR *Castle* Class 4-6-0 No 7029 *Clun Castle* pounds up Hatton bank with the northbound *'Zulu'*, a name once applied to an express service on this route. So far as the author is concerned the beginning of the end of these through services came on 9th September 1962 when his beloved *Kings* were withdrawn from this route. (T.R.Amos)

MOUNT/EVANS

SECRET

somebody isn't using his intelligence...

KEEP OUR SECRETS SECRET

ISSUED BY H.M. GOVERNMENT

Printed for Her Majesty's Stationery Office by M.M.P. Ltd. Dd.167604

KEEP OUR SECRETS SECRET, 1965, REGINALD MOUNT AND EILEEN M. EVANS. HM GOVERNMENT

In an atmosphere already heavy with Cold War paranoia, the 1950s and early 1960s saw a series of trials and defections of Soviet spies, provoking alarm in official circles at the extent of the Soviet Union's infiltration into the armed forces, the Civil Service and the Security Service. In response, in May 1961 the government appointed Lord Radcliffe to chair an inquiry into security procedures in the Public Service. Following publication of the committee's report, in April 1962, the Central Office of Information commissioned a series of posters – more than a hundred different designs were produced over the next few years – with the aim of improving security. Most of them, like this one, used the slogan 'Keep our secrets secret'. Although the 'spy problem' receded in the later 1960s, the necessity for continuing security education was made evident by the loss of a Child Benefit database by HM Revenue and Customs in 2007, and subsequent information and security breaches. Reginald Mount (1906–79) and Eileen M. Evans (1921–2006) had begun working together at the Ministry of Information in the war and later formed the Mount/Evans studio.

The Woman who wouldn't

The Woman Who Wouldn't said, " I
Have a pretty good time on the sly,
It's easy to cheat
With light, petrol and heat,
As for *savings* or *work*—I don't try."

The Woman Who Wouldn't said, " Queues
Are terribly hard on the shoes
But Black Market shopping
Is not. There's no stopping
Me shopping wherever I choose."

The Woman Who Wouldn't said, " Who
Is smarter than I am ?—not *you*,
Wasting time stopping waste—
Why, I couldn't be faced
With such wasteful, distasteful todo."

But all thanks to the women like You,
To the millions who Would and who Do,
Not selfishly spending,
But saving and mending
And working to see Britain through.

REPRINT OF 'REPORT TO THE WOMEN OF BRITAIN' Nº 12. ISSUED BY HIS MAJESTY'S GOVERNMENT

PRINTED FOR H.M. STATIONERY OFFICE BY FOSH & CROSS LTD., LONDON 51/3872

THE WOMAN WHO WOULDN'T, LATE 1940s. HM GOVERNMENT

The vilification of the 'Woman Who Wouldn't' formed part of a government campaign against waste and the temptations of the black market in the years of postwar austerity. Rationing continued into the 1950s and posters like this that encouraged thrift and 'working to see Britain through' were used to temper unrealistic expectations. The wording also reveals a shift in attitude towards the role of women: they were no longer called to the factories, but were asked to return to their domestic duties and to carry them out with one eye on the benefit this would bring to the nation.

YOU work in LEAD

E · SHEET · PLATE
MPOUNDS · STRIP · PIPES · SHOT · FOIL
OYS · BATTERIES · WHITE LEAD · COMPOUNDS · CABLE · S
STRIP · PLATE · SHEET · SOLDER · ALLOYS · PIPES
SHOT · FOIL · SOLD

MARSHALL AID ENDS 1952

As each month goes by we must pay for more of what we need by our exports of manufactured goods

!

Prepared for His Majesty's Government by the Economic Information Unit and the Central Office of Information.

A6693 Wt.35749 10,000 12/49 Gp.961 Fosh & Cross Ltd., London.

YOU WORK IN LEAD, 1949. THE ECONOMIC INFORMATION UNIT AND THE CENTRAL OFFICE OF INFORMATION

'American dollars saved the world', according to historian Michael J. Hogan, referring to the Marshall Plan (European Recovery Program) that pumped much-needed US aid into the devastated countries of Western Europe in the years 1948–52. Fearful that postwar instability would be fertile ground for the spread of Communist ideology, the United States government gave in the region of $13 billion dollars and provided vital technical assistance to sixteen nations in this period. Marshall Aid boosted Western Europe's economic recovery, but the governments of the recipient countries, such as Britain, were keenly aware that they had to prepare for the time when the ERP ended. Posters like this one graphically brought home the message, just one year into the programme.

Yorkshire's best is the world's best and it gets us the goods we want most

Come on Yorkshire!

LET'S GET SPINNING
LET'S GET WEAVING

Printed for H.M. Stationery Office by Stafford & Co., Ltd., Netherfield, Nottingham. 51-702.

Issued by the Ministry of Labour and National Service and the Board of Trade.

LET'S GET SPINNING, LET'S GET WEAVING, *c.* LATE 1940s. MINISTRY OF LABOUR AND NATIONAL SERVICE AND THE BOARD OF TRADE

In order to reduce the postwar balance of payments deficit, whereby Britain was spending more on imports, particularly food, than it was earning by exporting manufactured goods, the government was keen to encourage those industries whose products could be sold overseas. Among them was the Yorkshire textile industry, which had an international reputation stretching back to its heyday in the nineteenth century. The export of cotton and wool products helped to pay for food from the countries and territories in the Commonwealth, such as Australia, New Zealand and the West Indies, as well as from the United States and elsewhere, represented in this poster by the men queuing up with their produce before the John Bull-type figure displaying a roll of cloth.

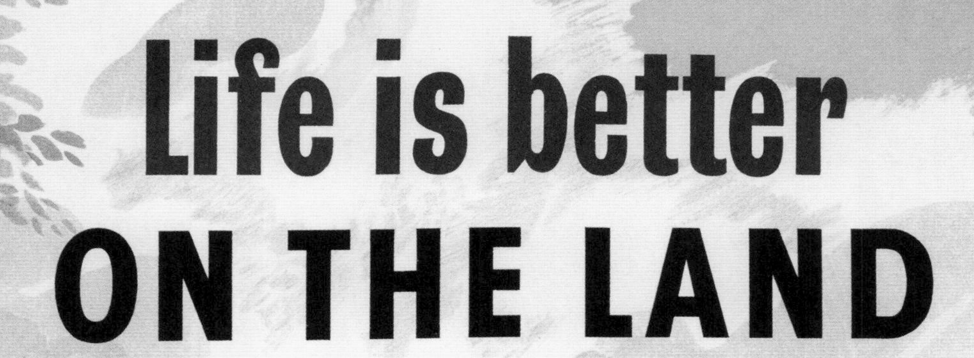

Good permanent jobs for
skilled workers.
Free training with
allowances for newcomers

Ask your local Employment Exchange

P.P. 233

ISSUED BY THE MINISTRY OF LABOUR AND NATIONAL SERVICE

Printed for H.M.Stationery Office by ALF BOLTON, LIVERPOOL 3

LIFE IS BETTER ON THE LAND, *c.*1950s, PATTEN. MINISTRY OF LABOUR AND NATIONAL SERVICE

In the postwar era, the government used public information posters to try and influence ordinary people's choice of work. The aim was to channel workers into Britain's undermanned industries and therefore to help promote a speedy recovery from the war. The country was far from self-sufficient in food, a situation that was exacerbated by poor harvests in 1946 and 1947 and the necessity to feed people in the areas of Europe under British control. This meant an over-dependence on imported produce and the continuance of food rationing until 1954. The 'Life is better on the land' campaign hoped to entice people into farming in order to improve the country's agricultural output.

LEWITT-HIM

P.R.D. 242

POST EARLY AND DON'T MISS THE 'NOON' POST, JAN LE WITT AND GEORGE HIM. GPO (GENERAL POST OFFICE)

On the eve of the Second World War in 1939, over 7 billion letters were delivered in Britain each year. The number continued to grow after the conflict, reaching 10 billion in 1960. However, it was during the war years that signs of the nanny state first emerged in the postal service. Prompted by the high volume of military communication by mail and telegraph, ordinary people were exhorted to 'post early' in the hope of easing the strain on the GPO. It was thought that if enough people heeded this advice, the Post Office would receive a steady stream of mail to sort and deliver, rather than being overwhelmed at the end of the day. The Polish-born artists Jan Le Witt (1907–91) and George Him (1900–81) came to London in 1937 and designed posters for the Ministry of Information and the GPO, illustrated children's books and created murals for the Festival of Britain in 1951. The partnership was dissolved in 1954.

REGINALD MOUNT

June

HELP EVERYBODY

There's more room remember in June and September

July · August

STAGGERED HOLIDAYS

September

P.P.153

PRINTED FOR H.M. STATIONERY OFFICE BY G.C.M. PRINTING SERVICE LTD. LEICESTER 51-9110

STAGGERED HOLIDAYS HELP EVERYBODY, *c.*1950s, REGINALD MOUNT

The rigours of the Second World War and the austerity in its immediate aftermath had put paid to the idea of the holiday for the bulk of the population. In the late 1940s and early 1950s, this pent-up need for recreation was tapped into by entrepreneurs such as Billy Butlin and Fred Pontin, resulting in the golden age of the holiday camp. The success of these organizations, as well as a general rise in the number of holidaymakers, led to a government campaign to encourage a more even spread of visitors across the summer months to relieve the pressure placed on resorts and transport. Reginald Mount (1906–79) joined the Ministry of Information at the beginning of the Second World War and continued to do work for the Central Office of Information and a number of government agencies in the postwar era.

It's finer remember in June and September

STAGGER YOUR HOLIDAYS, *c.*1950s

With increasing prosperity in the 1950s, and provision for paid holidays for the working class made by the Holiday Pay Act of 1938, the numbers frequenting the British seaside resorts in July and August became considerable. A further factor in the overcrowding were customs such as the Welsh 'Miners' Fortnight' at the end of July and beginning of August when the pits closed for routine maintenance and to give the colliery workers a break. To cope with the problem, the government used posters like this to influence the dates people chose to go on holiday. With the same intent, after a trial period in 1965–70, the August Bank Holiday was moved by Act of Parliament in 1971 from the first to the last Monday in the month. However, by that time, the rise of the package holiday meant the seaside towns the government wished to protect were already in decline.

GET RID OF THAT BOTTLENECK

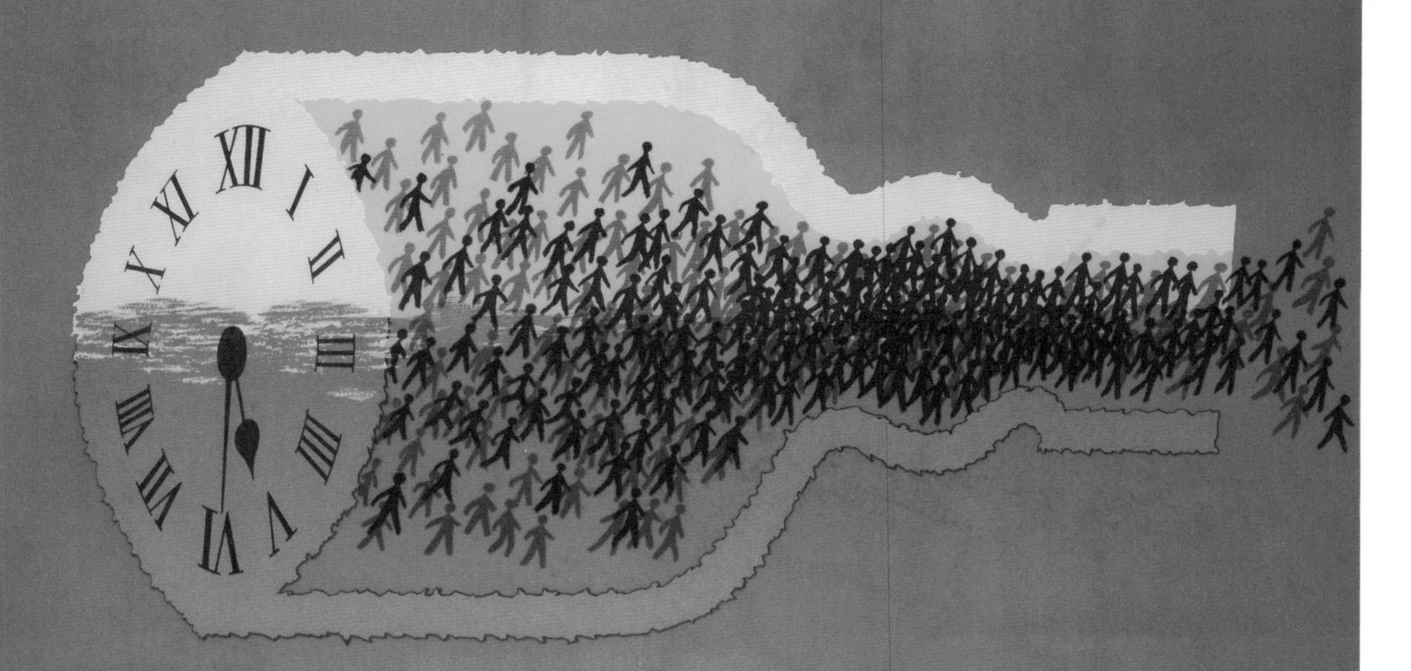

BY STAGGERING WORKING HOURS

REGINALD MOUNT

Prepared by the Central Office of Information for the Ministry of Transport and Civil Aviation.

A1604 Wt.40337 3M 8/57 Gp.961 F. & C. Ltd.

GET RID OF THAT BOTTLENECK, 1957, REGINALD MOUNT. MINISTRY OF TRANSPORT AND AVIATION

Following the successful trial of staggered working hours in certain cities in France, the Minister of Transport appointed a committee in 1956 to consider ways of staggering the hours people worked in London. Posters such as this one were produced but the campaign met with resistance from employers who thought a change to the standard nine-to-five routine would impinge on efficiency and make it difficult to recruit staff. By 1961, only 57,000 out of the 1 million people who travelled to London each day were working staggered hours. Reginald Mount (1906–79) worked for the Ministry of Information in the Second World War and for the Central Office of Information in the postwar era. He also designed the poster for the Ealing comedy film *The Ladykillers* (1955).

4 RULES FOR A *Happy Smile*

The HAPPY SMILE • DENTAL HEALTH CAMPAIGN •

1 Eat nourishing meals, with no sweet, sticky snacks in between.

Eat good food no sticky mush;

2 Brush your teeth regularly, after breakfast and last thing at night.

Both morn and night, please use the brush;

3 Finish meals with a cleansing food like an apple, when brushing is not possible.

An apple's best your meal to end;

4 Visit your dentist regularly, to keep your teeth and gums healthy.

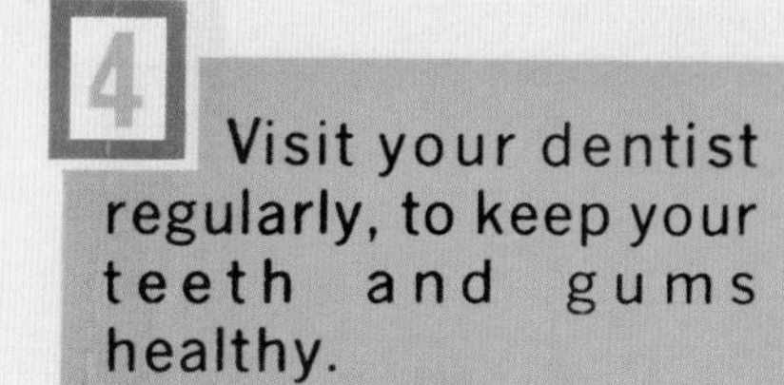

And see the dentist—he's your friend!

PREPARED FOR THE SCOTTISH HOME AND HEALTH DEPARTMENT BY THE CENTRAL OFFICE OF INFORMATION.

PRINTED FOR H.M. STATIONERY OFFICE BY McCORQUODALE & CO. LTD. GLASGOW 53-2318

FOUR RULES FOR A HAPPY SMILE, 1960s. SCOTTISH HOME AND HEALTH DEPARTMENT

With the establishment of the National Health Service in 1948, dental examination and treatment was made available for free. As demand surged, the expense of this service was soon felt, with budgets stretched beyond initial estimates. The fees paid to dentists were cut and in 1952 charges were introduced, which, coupled with the end of sweet and sugar rationing in 1953, meant that the percentage of children without any evidence of tooth decay fell from 22 per cent in 1948 to just 13 per cent in 1958. The 'Happy Smile' campaign hoped to reverse this downward trend.

THE SEVEN RULES OF HEALTH

You and your family will stand a better chance of avoiding colds, influenza and other common ailments—as well as more serious diseases such as tuberculosis—if you follow these simple rules. The rules offer the best guidance on how to improve your health and increase your vitality.

Rule 1 — FRESH AIR

Sleep, eat and, if it is possible, work in airy rooms.

Headaches, lack of appetite, and that tired feeling are often due to a stuffy atmosphere.

Rule 2 — EXERCISE

Rule 3 — SLEEP..

See that the children—whatever their age—get enough sleep...

And you, too! Don't forget to open the windows and draw back the curtains

A GUIDE TO YOUR CHILD'S SLEEP

BABIES UNDER 2 need about 16 hours sleep in 24.

CHILDREN UP TO 5 need about 12 to 14 hours, so should be in bed by 6 p.m.

CHILDREN OF 5 TO 7 need about 12 hours, so should be in bed by 7 p.m.

CHILDREN OF 7 TO 11 need about 11 hours sleep, which means bed by about 8 p.m.

UP TO THE AGE OF 16 boys and girls need 9 to 10 hrs. sleep each night.

Rule 4 — ABOUT CLOTHING

Let's be comfortable

Rule 5 — KEEPING CLEAN

BRUSH YOUR HAIR night and morning, and remember that it needs washing quite often.

ALWAYS CLEAN TEETH after meals. No sweets or biscuits after teeth are cleaned at bed-time.

WASH YOUR HANDS before meals; always remember to wash them after using the W.C.

WASH ALL OVER every day. It takes a bit of time but it's worth it, and so refreshing.

Rule 6 — CONCERNING FOOD

A balanced diet

Meat, milk, fish, eggs or cheese needed for body building;
Fruit, vegetables or salads essential for a healthy skin;
Bread, flour, potatoes, sugar or fats supply your energy;
YOU NEED FOOD FROM EACH GROUP EVERY DAY

Concerning Food — HANDLING FOOD

It's very important to have clean hands when preparing your meals; important for the health of the family

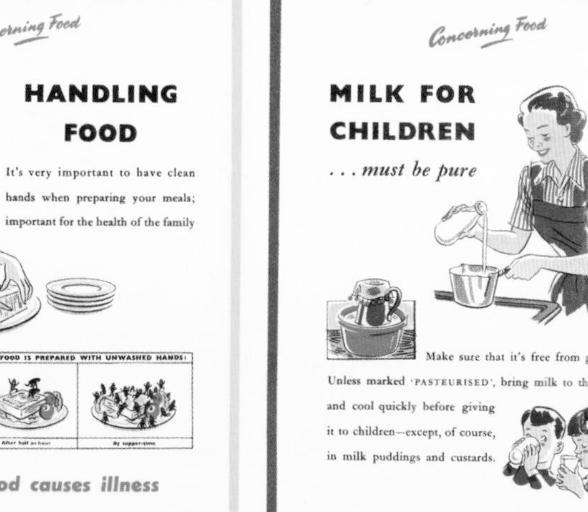

Infected food causes illness

Concerning Food — MILK FOR CHILDREN

...must be pure

Make sure that it's free from germs. Unless marked 'PASTEURISED', bring milk to the boil and cool quickly before giving it to children—except, of course, in milk puddings and custards.

Rule 7 — LEISURE—enrich your life

with spare time interests

PREVENTION IS BETTER THAN CURE —— LET THE RULES BECOME HABITS

Prepared for the MINISTRY OF HEALTH and the DEPARTMENT OF HEALTH FOR SCOTLAND by the Central Office of Information

Printed by Multi Machine Plates Ltd., London

THE SEVEN RULES OF HEALTH, *c.* EARLY 1950s. MINISTRY OF HEALTH AND DEPARTMENT OF HEALTH FOR SCOTLAND

This poster uses the slogan 'Prevention is better than cure' in an attempt to persuade people to adopt a healthier lifestyle. It is undated but is probably from the early 1950s. At that time it was hoped that by improving the general health of the nation the cost of running the National Health Service could be reduced; in 1952, just four years after the foundation of the NHS, dental and prescription charges were introduced. The poster includes some sound advice, such as 'Wash all over every day. It takes a bit of time but it's worth it, and so refreshing'. These suggestions were not only aimed at tackling the common cold and influenza but also at preventing the spread of serious diseases such as tuberculosis. In 1950, there were 50,000 cases of TB in the UK, but the number began to decline with better nutrition and housing, the pasteurization of milk, the use of antibiotics and the introduction of the BCG vaccine in 1953.

Hey!

time I was immunised against Diphtheria

Ask your family doctor or at your Welfare Centre

D.06 Prepared for the Ministry of Health by the Central Office of Information

HEY! TIME I WAS IMMUNISED AGAINST DIPHTHERIA, *c.*1950s.
MINISTRY OF HEALTH

Diphtheria is a highly contagious bacterial disease that mostly affects the nose and throat. It can lead to difficulties breathing and ultimately suffocation through swelling or obstruction of the throat. In the 1930s, diphtheria was third in the list of causes of death in children in England and Wales and in 1940 more than 61,000 cases were reported in the whole of the UK, resulting in 3,283 deaths. With people crowded together in shelters during the Second World War, fears about the spread of the disease led to the start of a nationally coordinated programme of immunization for everyone under the age of fifteen. The campaign, of which posters such as this one were a part, was extremely successful, so that in 1957 there were just thirty-eight cases of the disease and six deaths.

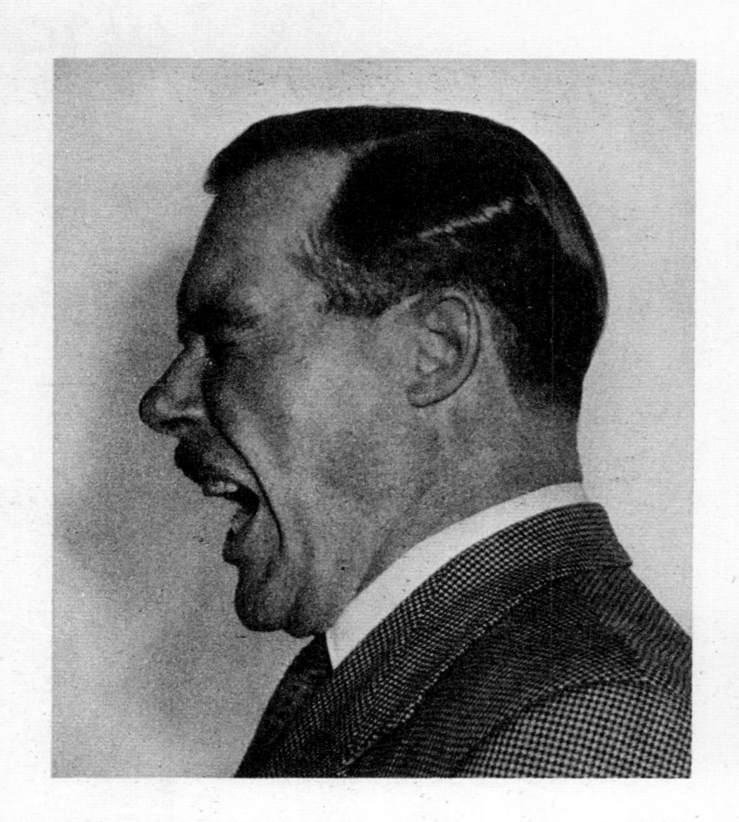

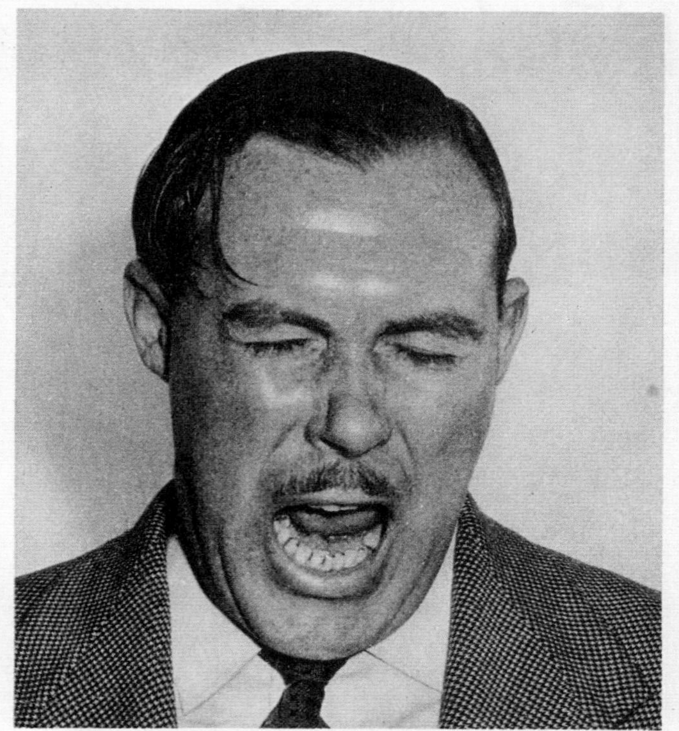

WANTED

... a handkerchief

COUGHS & SNEEZES SPREAD DISEASES

Trap the germs in your handkerchief

M.M.P LTD Wt P10435-0959

PREPARED FOR THE MINISTRY OF HEALTH BY THE CENTRAL OFFICE OF INFORMATION

COUGHS AND SNEEZES SPREAD DISEASES, *c.*1950s. MINISTRY OF HEALTH

Following its initial use in the Second World War, the 'Coughs and sneezes spread diseases' slogan has been used in a number of different health campaigns over the years and was employed in 2007 as part of an attempt to reduce the spread of influenza and other diseases by the National Director of Pandemic Influenza Preparedness. All the posters convey the same basic message: use a handkerchief (or tissue in the modern-day version) to stop the spread of germs when you cough or sneeze. This design, probably from the 1950s, showing a man sneezing, has echoes in the image used on posters and leaflets issued by the National Health Service in relation to the swine-flu epidemic at the end of the first decade of the twenty-first century. It shows the power and endurance of a relatively simple combination of image and words.

STOP where's your handkerchief?

Ah, here it is!

that's the way – safe for everyone

COUGHS AND SNEEZES SPREAD DISEASES

Trap the germs in your handkerchief

ISSUED BY THE 

MINISTRY OF HEALTH

PRINTED FOR H.M. STATIONERY OFFICE BY J. WEINER LTD. LONDON, W.C.1. 51- 42 55

COUGHS AND SNEEZES SPREAD DISEASES. MINISTRY OF HEALTH

The 'Coughs and sneezes spread diseases' slogan was first used during the Second World War to combat absenteeism at a time when a healthy workforce was critical to the nation's survival. In the immediate postwar era the campaign was augmented by short films that were shown in cinemas, such as one that in an amusing way encouraged people to use a handkerchief properly. With labour shortages in the late 1940s and 1950s and the necessity to increase production for the sake of economic revival, the need for people not to be ill was still pertinent. Designers sought ways to convey the same message but in an eye-catching manner, such as the three colours of a traffic light used in this poster. The rhyming slogan proved to be so memorable that it is still part of today's lexicon.

WASH YOUR HANDS
BEFORE EATING
HOLIDAY HEALTH DEPENDS ON HOLIDAY HYGIENE
Prepared for the Scottish Home and Health Department by the Central Office of Information
PRINTED IN SCOTLAND FOR H.M. STATIONERY OFFICE BY GAVIN WATSON LTD., GLASGOW. 53-2599.

WASH YOUR HANDS BEFORE EATING, *c.* MID-1960s. SCOTTISH HOME AND HEALTH DEPARTMENT

As prosperity in Britain grew in the middle of the twentieth century so did the amount of disposable income, which led to a rise in family holidays and the purchasing of luxury items such as the portable barbecue illustrated here. The Holidays with Pay Act of 1938 gave every worker the entitlement to one week's paid holiday. By the 1950s, this had risen to two weeks for most people and continued to increase, and more thought was given as to how people would spend that time. It was considered important for the workforce to enjoy their well-earned time off with their families but equally vital that they return to work healthy and refreshed, and the promotion of hygienic practices went a long way to ensure that.

HOLIDAY HEALTH DEPENDS ON HOLIDAY HYGIENE

Wash your
hands
before eating

HOLIDAY HEALTH DEPENDS ON HOLIDAY HYGIENE, *c.* MID-1960s.
SCOTTISH HOME AND HEALTH DEPARTMENT

Following on from the popular 'Coughs and sneezes spread diseases' slogan first used in the Second World War, health and hygiene became a central theme of public information campaigns in the succeeding decades. To take the pressure off the National Health Service, the British public was encouraged to aspire to a healthier, outdoors lifestyle while maintaining good standards of hygiene. The message in posters such as this was clear: good hygiene is fundamental to all our aspirations, underpins family health and leads to idyllic summer holidays. The era's conception of a typical family is pictured making the most of what was considered important – the time, space and freedom to enjoy life to the full.

WASHING UP

1 SCRAPE...

into a bin, kept covered when not in use.

2 WASH...

in one part of double sink, using a detergent and changing water often.
Water temperature should be at least 110°F.

3 RINSE...

in other part of double sink.
Rinsing water should be at 170°F. or contain a chemical steriliser.

4 DRAIN...

and leave till dry.

COI Issued by the Ministry of Health

Printed for H.M. Stationery Office by M.M.P. Ltd. Wt. 56397-9979

WASHING UP, 1962. MINISTRY OF HEALTH

In 1848, following a severe outbreak of cholera and after campaigning by the Health of Towns Association and social reformers such as Edwin Chadwick, a Liberal government under Lord John Russell took the first steps to ameliorate the sanitary conditions of towns by passing a Public Health Act. That the state would implement measures to improve the health of the population or indeed might have a responsibility to its citizens to do so was highly controversial at that period. By the time of the publication of the Beveridge Report in 1942, which identified the five great evils of squalor, ignorance, want, idleness and disease, there was much more acceptance of government interference to remedy these ills. This led to the establishment of the welfare state after the war. Hygiene was a key factor in fighting squalor and disease and the Ministry of Health ran campaigns to educate the population in what might now seem rather basic routines.

CUT IT OUT
OR CUT IT DOWN

CIGARETTES HARM YOUR HEALTH

SM15a. ISSUED BY THE MINISTRY OF HEALTH

Printed for H.M. Stationery Office by Fosh & Cross Ltd., London. Wt. P.10650

CIGARETTES HARM YOUR HEALTH, 1962–63, REGINALD MOUNT. MINISTRY OF HEALTH

In comparison to contemporary messages on cigarette packets (Smoking Kills; Smoking may reduce the blood flow and cause impotence), this government message from the early 1960s seems relatively mild. Nonetheless, the campaign against smoking slowly had the desired effect: 51 per cent of men smoked cigarettes in 1974 compared with 65 per cent in the late 1940s. Reginald Mount (1906–79) worked initially for the Ministry of Information during the Second World War and later for the Central Office of Information.

MOUNT EVANS

DON'T ASK A MAN TO DRINK AND DRIVE

ISSUED BY H.M. GOVERNMENT. Printed for Her Majesty's Stationery Office by Stafford & Co. Ltd. Nottingham. 51/5789 (11/66)

DON'T ASK A MAN TO DRINK AND DRIVE, 1966, REGINALD MOUNT AND EILEEN M. EVANS. HM GOVERNMENT

This poster was published in the same year as the Road Safety Bill (enacted in 1967), which made it an offence for drivers to have more than a prescribed limit of 80 mg of alcohol per 100 ml of blood. The legislation also made provision for the introduction of the hand-held breathalyzer device so that police officers could test a driver's BAC (blood alcohol concentration) level at the roadside. Prior to that, those motorists suspected of having drunk too much alcohol were asked to walk in a straight line (often using the road markings as a guide), on the basis that alcohol decreases motor function and therefore makes walking in a controlled fashion difficult. The white lines running vertically down the centre of this poster allude both to the road-related message and to the walking test. The wording not only reveals how at the time it was expected that a man in a couple would drive, but also suggests that excessive consumption of alcohol was perceived to be a predominantly male problem. Reginald Mount (1906–79) and Eileen M. Evans (1921–2006) had worked together at the Ministry of Information and the Central Office of Information before establishing the Mount/Evans studio.

GET FIT FOR THE ROAD
REGINALD MOUNT
WEAR A HELMET
ALWAYS
ISSUED BY THE MINISTRY OF TRANSPORT
Printed for H.M. Stationery Office by M.M.P. Ltd., London Wt.42317-4/63-2993
COI

GET FIT FOR THE ROAD, 1963, REGINALD MOUNT. MINISTRY OF TRANSPORT

In 1935, T. E. Lawrence ('Lawrence of Arabia') was fatally injured in a motorcycle accident. Hugh Cairns, a young neurosurgeon who attended him, was so affected by the tragedy that he undertook research into this type of accident. He came to the conclusion that the wearing of crash helmets as standard would save many lives, but it was decades before this was enacted into law. Postwar, safety for motorcyclists became a more pressing issue as traffic – and accidents – increased, and the popularity of the Vespa and other motor scooters soared. This led the Ministry of Transport to run campaigns to persuade people to wear helmets voluntarily and posters such as this one by Reginald Mount (1906–79) were produced. However, it was not until 1973 that the wearing of motorcycle helmets became compulsory, although it is still a subject that provokes controversy.

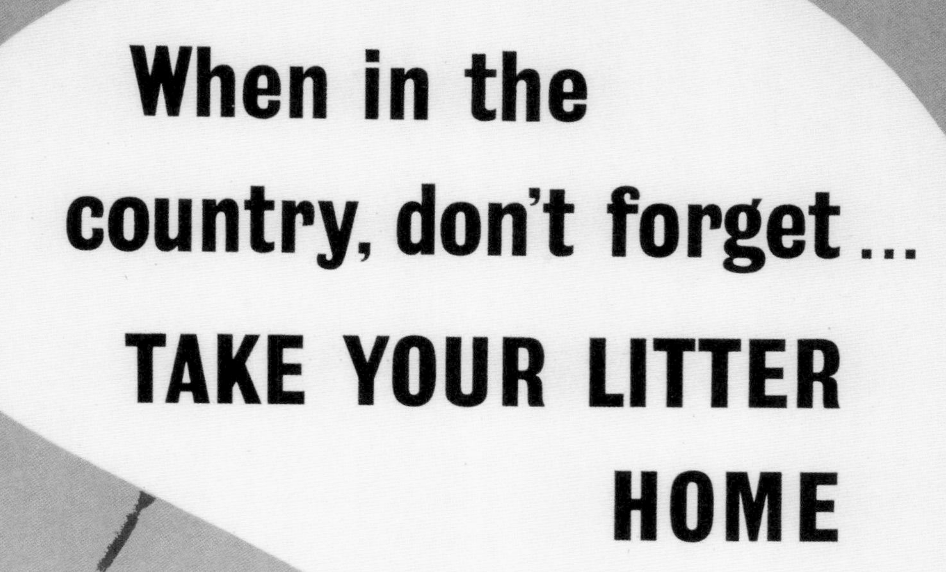

KEEP BRITAIN TIDY

AL. 574 Prepared for the Ministry of Housing and Local Government by the Central Office of Information

Printed for H.M. Stationery Office by Taylor Garnett Evans & Co. Ltd., Watford, Herts. 51-8724

KEEP BRITAIN TIDY, EARLY 1960s, REGINALD MOUNT. MINISTRY OF HOUSING AND LOCAL GOVERNMENT

In 1954, in response to the increasing amounts of litter everywhere, the National Federation of Women's Institutes, led by Lady Elizabeth Brunner, passed a resolution to 'Keep Britain Tidy'. The following year the Keep Britain Tidy Group was formed and in 1961 it became an independent organization and received government backing. It continues to campaign for cleaner, greener places to this day. It is hard to know at this point if the use of the red squirrel by the designer Reginald Mount (1906–79) was a deliberate choice to associate the fragility of the countryside with a species that was becoming endangered. Alternatively, it might simply have been a wish to use an animal that was appealing – just as a decade later The Wombles television characters were used in a Keep Britain Tidy poster campaign.

KEEP BRITAIN TIDY

Prepared for the Ministry of Housing and Local Government by the Central Office of Information

Printed for Her Majesty's Stationery Office by J. Weiner Ltd., Acton, W.3. 51-2369

KEEP BRITAIN TIDY, 1965, ROYSTON COOPER. MINISTRY OF HOUSING AND LOCAL GOVERNMENT

The Keep Britain Tidy campaign, which began in 1954 as a resolution passed by the National Federation of Women's Institutes, became an independent organization in 1961 and started to receive its first official government funding. Support also came in the form of posters commissioned by the Ministry of Housing and Local Government, such as this one. The image of the pelican, with a large amount of rubbish in its throat pouch, is both a witty reminder to people to take their litter home with them and a possible subliminal warning of the impact to wildlife from rubbish that had been thoughtlessly discarded. Royston Cooper (1931–85), a painter and typographer as well as a designer of posters, annual reports and packaging, had his own studio in north London for twenty-three years.

A. GAMES.
KEEP
BRITAIN
TIDY

KEEP BRITAIN TIDY, 1963, ABRAM GAMES. MINISTRY OF HOUSING AND LOCAL GOVERNMENT

The Keep Britain Tidy Group was formed in 1955 by the National Federation of Women's Institutes following a resolution passed the year before. Its campaign was launched in response to the increasing 'throwaway culture' of the 1950s, which was resulting in litter defiling both urban and rural landscapes. In 1961, it became an independent organization and received its first official government funding. As the Britannia-like pose of the roadsweeper and the red, white and blue colours of the wheel of his cart indicate, Keep Britain Tidy's campaigns of this period often appealed to national pride to encourage people to dispose of their litter in a responsible way. Abram Games (1914–96) established his reputation as a leading poster designer during the Second World War, when he was an Official War Artist, and his postwar work included designing the logo for the Festival of Britain in 1951.

HELP BRITAIN SAVE
£5,000,000 A YEAR!

BUY BRITISH GOODS

BUY BRITISH GOODS, *c.*1968

The origins of the Buy British Goods slogan lay in the Buy Empire and Buy British campaigns run by the Empire Marketing Board in the period 1926–33 in order to boost empire trade. The need to encourage the public to Buy British arose once again in the mid-1960s when the Labour government under Harold Wilson faced a severe balance of payments crisis. In November 1967, it became necessary to devalue the pound; the aim was to sell more goods abroad by making them cheaper and more competitive in overseas markets. In parallel, the Buy British Goods campaign was intended to reduce the nation's dependence on foreign imports. Posters such as this one emphasized how an everyday activity such as food shopping could contribute to the economic health of the country.

STAN KROL
BE REALLY COOL
-MAN-
SAVE
POST OFFICE SAVINGS BANK

BE REALLY COOL, MAN, SAVE, 1964, STAN KROL

In the early 1960s, a campaign to encourage people to save with the Post Office Savings Bank tried a number of different approaches. In this poster, the appeal was made to a younger generation who were swept up in the wave of pop music created by bands such as the Beatles and the manner of speaking that was crossing the Atlantic from the USA. As part of the design, the POSB logo of a key topped with a crown has been cleverly adapted and incorporated into the guitar. Stan Krol (1910–85) was born into a Jewish family in Poland and initially studied chemistry. Arriving in England at the beginning of the war, he served in the army and subsequently became a graphic designer. He began to work for the GPO in the late 1940s and his clients also included BOAC, the United Nations Association and RoSPA.

Modernise your home and pay only a quarter of the cost with a House Improvement Grant.

For a 75% grant work must be finished by 23rd June 1973.
Work completed after this date qualifies for a 50% grant.

Ask for details at your Council Office.

Issued by the Welsh Office.

MODERNISE YOUR HOME, *c.*1971. WELSH OFFICE

By the terms of the Housing Act of 1971 the Conservative government under Edward Heath hoped to give a short, sharp boost to economic activity in 'assisted areas' such as Wales by offering grants covering 75 per cent of the cost of home improvements for a limited period of two years. At that time, 47 per cent of housing stock in the principality had been built before 1918 and many of these were back-to-back dwellings with no indoor toilet or bathroom, hot water or central heating. Simultaneously, thousands of houses were being demolished under slum clearance measures, the private housing market was collapsing because of the rise in mortgage interest rates and there was a shortage of new council houses – in 1972 and 1973 fewer council houses were built in Wales than in any year since 1946. As a result, the grants proved very popular and some 28,000 homes were improved in Wales in 1972 under the scheme; indeed, builders were so overwhelmed that the deadline of 23 June 1973 for completion of the work had to be extended. Housing was not the only thing being modernized in this era, the tea towel hanging on the wall in the poster shows the coins introduced for decimalization of the currency in February 1971.

THE POSTER & THE NANNY STATE

'In the case of nutrition and health, just as in the case of education, the gentleman in Whitehall really does know better what is good for people than the people know themselves.' These were the words penned by Labour politician Douglas Jay in *The Socialist Case* in 1937 to justify greater government intervention in the lives of ordinary people.

The notion that 'the man in Whitehall knows best' is hugely controversial and cuts right to the heart of debates between Labour and Conservative politicians about the appropriate size and role of the state. Traditionally, Labour supporters have emphasized the central importance of the state in solving society's ills, while Conservative adherents focus on the part played by the individual and personal responsibility. It is therefore not surprising that the pejorative term 'nanny state' was coined by a Conservative MP, Iain Macleod. Since its first usage in a column he wrote in the *Spectator* in 1965, this term has been widely adopted to mean excessive action on the part of the state to protect, govern or control particular aspects of society. This collection of posters has no such political agenda. Instead, *Keep Britain Tidy* both illuminates the concerns of successive postwar governments and reveals the various ways in which the state has sought to get its message across to the masses.

The Second World War dramatically changed the relationship between people and state in Britain. The extensive bombing of Britain's cities and the very real threat of a German invasion meant that the war reached far more intrusively into the lives of civilians than had been the case in the Great War. It was these unprecedented circumstances that led to the expansion of the role of the state. The British had entered the war as a moral crusade; they had taken on Fascism to fight for a better world. In part a reward for the sacrifices made in wartime, and in part a step towards making this 'better world' a reality, the postwar Labour government under Clement Attlee acted upon recommendations made by the British economist and social reformer William Beveridge in the so-called Beveridge Report (*Social Insurance and Allied Services*) of 1942. This led to the establishment of the modern welfare state. Gone would be the days of filthy, dirty back streets and half-starved children. Politicians promised a new Britain in which everyone, no matter what class, would be properly clothed and fed, and care would extend from the cradle to the grave.[1]

This optimistic vision of the postwar world was to be disseminated through the continued use of government propaganda in peacetime. During the Second World War the British authorities had used posters successfully to promote patriotism and a sense of duty in the population: men had been mobilized to fight and women had been urged to hold the home front together.[2] And it was this effective use of the poster to moderate behaviour in wartime Britain that paved the way for its role in communicating collective social goals once the fighting was over.[3] Indeed, the Official Committee on the Machinery of Government insisted in August 1944 that the existing public-relations departments within Whitehall be preserved at the end of war, explaining that 'their functions, if properly conceived, are useful and indeed essential in modern government'.[4] And thus state intervention in the lives of ordinary people, which had been a response to an emergency situation, became a permanent feature of the relationship between the state and individual in the second half of the twentieth century.

In spite of the evident successes of the propaganda poster in wartime, politicians in the early postwar years remained reluctant to be directly associated with issuing public information posters. Though regarded as expedient when the country was fighting for its survival, designing propaganda posters to aid governmental policy in peacetime seemed to fall dangerously close to the activities of commercial advertisers. Ministers came to terms with their uneasiness about this mode of communication by relying on voluntary organizations and local-government workers to produce the posters. Designing visual communication and bringing it before the public with the aim of influencing its behaviour had not traditionally been part of central government's activities in times of peace.[5] This, and the fact that propaganda posters were closely associated with Hitler and Mussolini's dictatorships, explains why ministers were initially reluctant to embrace this powerful means of conveying messages to the general population.

Posters first came on the scene in continental Europe in the 1860s. Assisted by the mechanization of printing and fuelled by growing literacy rates across the continent, there was a proliferation of this new mode of communication. Centuries earlier, prints made from wood engravings had informed ordinary people about the spread of disease, among other things, and following on from this, broadsides, which were single sheets of paper, disseminated news and public notices. But when the poster first appeared on the streets of Paris in the late nineteenth century, it was visually commanding in a totally new way.[6] Unlike works of art, which were to be viewed with care and consideration, public information posters were to be read at speed. And in contrast to paintings, posters aimed to communicate information that would alter the viewer's behaviour. For the poster's message to stay with its readers, it needed to offer an arresting and memorable combination of pictures and words. Cyril Bird, the creator of the famous wartime posters with the slogan 'Careless talk costs lives', pinpointed the three key characteristics in human nature that had to be overcome: 'Firstly a general aversion to reading any notice of any sort, secondly a general disinclination to believe that any notice, even if it was read, can possibly be addressed to oneself; thirdly, a general unwillingness, even so, to remember the message long enough to do anything about it.'[7]

The poster had many iterations following its inception. Early posters relied on sketches and cartoons to illustrate the information they conveyed. Indeed, it was only in the 1940s that photographs could be incorporated into designs. And initially the photographs used on posters were black and white and became grainy when blown up to scale.[8] As production methods developed, however, colourful images came to take centre stage. Designers juxtaposed eye-catching visuals with minimal text in their work, and they deliberately sought to provoke an emotional response from their audiences, be it laughter, shock, fear or shame. A perfect combination of these factors delivered the chosen message in a memorable way, which was essential to making people improve their habits.

However, whether demonizing, satirizing or praising behaviour, by the late 1960s the poster had begun to

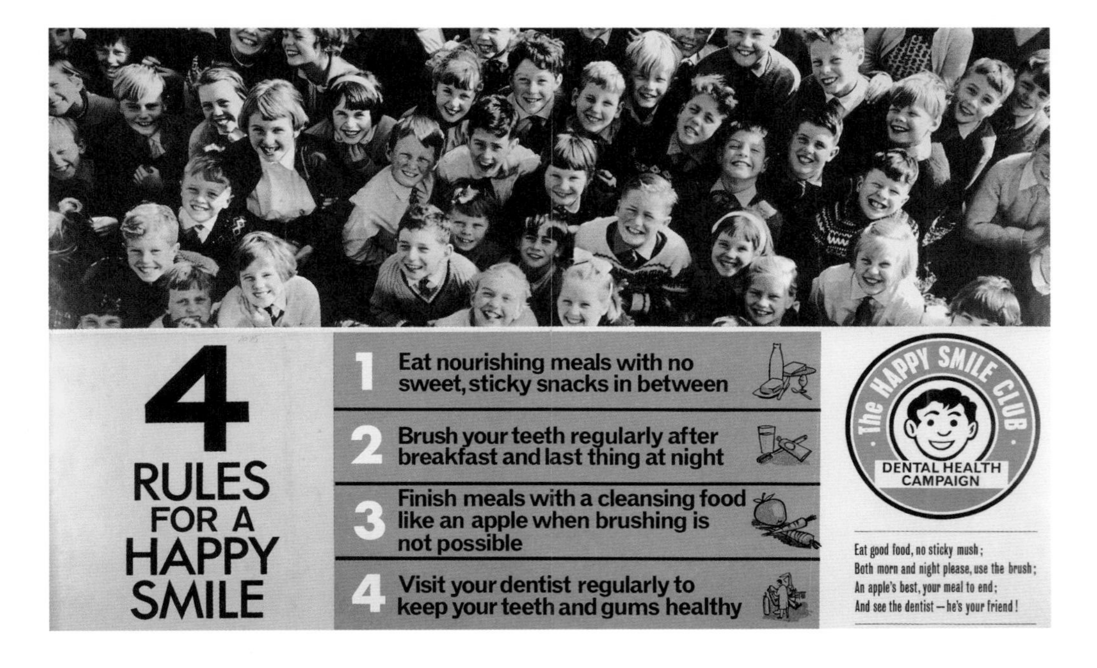

Created for a dental-health campaign run by the Scottish Home and Health Department in the 1960s, this poster formed part of a continuous effort by the authorities to protect the teeth of Scotland's children that had begun with the passing of the Education (Scotland) Act of 1908.

lose its power to offer a unique and compelling 'visual shorthand'[9] as television ownership became much more mainstream (95 per cent of households had TV sets by 1969).[10] Nonetheless, between the 1860s and the 1970s, the ever-evolving poster occupied an extremely important position within visual culture. And it was towards the end of the poster's heyday, between 1945 and the 1970s, that the British government adopted this medium of communication to build a better Britain.

Public information posters offer us fascinating insights into the changing concerns of central government in the recent past. Every poster had an agenda: In 1945, for example, a food crisis struck, triggering a series of posters designed to modify the British public's consumption. 'Eat less bread' was the slogan of one of the first campaigns following the conclusion of the Second World War. Mere months after the end of hostilities it became clear that there was a lack of food across the globe. The war itself was in part to blame, but this was compounded by natural causes, including the failure of the monsoon in India. The result was a major shortage of wheat and rice. A shortfall of five millions tons of wheat from world supplies compelled the government to take action at home. British citizens were told 'Bread means lives. Don't waste a crumb' and posters advised 'Go easy with bread. Eat potatoes instead.'[11]

By the end of 1945, however, getting the British economy back on track was a central motive of the government. The war had put the country's finances under enormous strain. During the conflict, the state had relied on war bonds and other public saving schemes to underwrite the war effort. Saving schemes were just as important in peacetime as the government struggled to pay off the nation's war debts and rebuild the economy. Public information posters therefore called on people to invest their money in what came to be called National Savings.

Just as the government tried to influence where ordinary people put their money, so too did it try to affect people's choice of work as part of its plans to promote a speedy recovery. In 1939, Britain's industries had shifted onto a wartime footing, focusing on the production of munitions rather than consumer goods. With the end of hostilities, the demand for weapons understandably collapsed. To increase the nation's exports and thereby redress the balance of trade, the government required members of the labour force to move into those industries that had overseas markets, such as textiles and metal work. Accordingly, campaigns hoping to lure workers into the wool and cotton trades tried to make the industry look like an attractive prospect.[12]

It was not only the textile industries that saw propaganda posters as a way to soothe their troubles at the end of the war. The General Post Office (GPO) also sought to persuade letter-writers and parcel-senders to act in ways that would improve the efficiency and profits of the Post Office. It ran a campaign encouraging people to 'post early' in the hope that it would receive a steady stream of mail to sort and deliver, rather than being overwhelmed towards the end of the day. The GPO also launched a series of posters educating users about the correct way to package up a parcel. Although the GPO had been steadily increasing its mechanical capacity between 1920 and 1950, a number of factors including inflation and economic recession conspired to mean that it ran at a loss. The GPO therefore used posters to advertise the range of services they offered, such as air mail, in the hope of reversing its fortunes.[13]

Alongside concerns about the state of the British economy, health was a major postwar preoccupation. Spurred on by the recommendations of the Beveridge Report, the National Health Service was established in 1948, offering a brighter future for all those who had put their lives on the line for Britain during the conflict. However, the NHS was not simply a reward for wartime gallantry. There were economic imperatives, too. A healthy nation was a productive nation: a population free from disease could make a decisive contribution to building a prosperous society. Wartime posters had encouraged Britons to adopt lifestyles that would make them 'fighting fit'. Postwar posters had similar goals.

Right from the start, the NHS sought to educate the public about the dangers of contagion. 'Coughs and sneezes spread diseases' was a mantra dating back to the war and due to the catchiness of its rhyme it has been used ever since to raise awareness about spreading germs. Posters on this subject depict hapless sneezers who pose a menace to others around them. Continuing the theme of preventing infection, public information posters after the war also encouraged parents to get their children immunized against diseases such as diphtheria. And so-called 'war aphrodisia' led to the rampant spread of venereal diseases in the 1940s, prompting a government campaign to raise awareness of their dangers. By the 1960s there was also a growing awareness of the harmful consequences of smoking, triggering a series of posters to discourage the habit, particularly among young people.[14]

In addition to boosting the economy and influencing the nation's health, public information posters were used to improve the environment. In the mid-1950s, recovery from the Second World War began to give way to mass consumerism. One of the consequences of the consumer boom was a significant rise in the amount of litter discarded on the streets. Keen to reduce the impact of littering, the National Federation of Women's Institutes initiated the 'Keep Britain Tidy' campaign in the 1950s. The Ministry of Housing and Local Government later supported this message via a series of posters produced by the Central Office of Information (which was formed in 1946 and succeeded the Ministry of Information).

While the 'Keep Britain Tidy' campaign encouraged ordinary people to be aware of their environment in one sense, road-safety posters urged people to be aware of their surroundings in another way. Road safety first became a concern during the First World War when the blackout enforced in urban areas caused a jump in the number of accidents between cars and pedestrians. The forerunner of the Royal Society for the Prevention of Accidents (RoSPA) was established in 1916 in response to these incidents (the name was changed in 1941). Throughout the rest of the century, this organization created shocking posters that emphasized both the consequences of making a mistake on the road and the possibility of avoiding such outcomes by following some simple rules.[15] When petrol rationing ended in 1950, RoSPA redoubled its efforts, aware that children had grown used to playing in streets that now saw an increase in traffic.[16]

In 1961, RoSPA set up the Tufty Club with the specific aim of improving road safety among children under five. By 1972, over two million children were members of local Tufty Clubs, where they heard about how Tufty and his friends were taught to cross the road safely by Mrs Owl. Road safety remained a serious

concern in the 1970s as road layouts became more complex. The Green Cross Code, for example, was introduced in 1970, and its campaign of 1976, with comics featuring the Green Cross Code Man, sought to address the dangers posed by growing numbers of cars on the road. Alongside this, the 'Clunk Click Every Trip' posters (and public information films) from the 1970s encouraged the use of seatbelts in cars, paving the way for this to become compulsory (in front seats) in 1983.

From the end of the Second World War, the British state increasingly used public information posters to inform, guide and alter the behaviour of ordinary people. The posters in this book have been selected from an extensive collection held in The National Archives and provide a unique insight into the thinking of the 'gentleman in Whitehall' over a period of thirty years from 1945. They reveal the various techniques employed to help people help themselves as well as reflecting the changing concerns of successive governments. Irrespective of the successes or failures of the individual campaigns, attitudes towards the 'nanny state' today remain as divided as ever.

Dr Hester Vaizey
THE NATIONAL ARCHIVES

1 William Crofts, *Coercion or Persuasion? Propaganda in Britain after 1945* (London, 1989), p. 10.
2 600, 000 British women were also recruited into non-combat jobs in the military within the Women's Royal Naval Service (WRNS or 'Wrens'), the Women's Auxiliary Force (WAAF or 'Waffs) and The Auxiliary Territorial Service (ATS).
3 Catherine Flood, *British Posters. Advertising, Art and Activism* (London, 2012), p. 175.
4 Mariel Grant, *Propaganda and the Role of the State in Inter-War Britain* (Oxford, 1994), p. 250.
5 Crofts, *Coercion or Persuasion?*, p. 1.
6 Paul Rennie, *Modern British Posters. Art, Design and Communication* (London, 2009), p. 1.
7 Philip M. Taylor, *Munitions of the Mind. A History of Propaganda from the Ancient World to the Present Day* (3rd edition, Manchester, 2003), p. 216.
8 Flood, *British Posters*, p. 26; Rennie, *Modern British Posters*, p. 116.
9 Flood, *British Posters*, p. 1.
10 Rennie, *Modern British Posters*, p. 175.
11 Crofts, *Coercion or Persuasion?*, pp. 99–101.
12 Ibid., p. 250.
13 Rennie, *Modern British Posters*, p. 51.
14 Flood, *British Posters*, p. 30.
15 Rennie, *Modern British Posters*, p. 146.
16 Flood, *British Posters*, p. 16.

ABOVE LEFT The Green Cross Code was launched by RoSPA in 1970 to improve road safety among pedestrians. Targeting young children in particular, the campaign used a costumed superhero called the Green Cross Man to get its message across.

ABOVE MIDDLE This shocking poster, with the hammer smashing a peach working as a metaphor for a car hitting a pedestrian's head, emphasizes both the high stakes of making a mistake on the road and the possibility of avoiding such outcomes by following some simple rules.

ABOVE RIGHT The 'Clunk Click Every Trip' slogan, with variants, was introduced in 1971 to encourage passengers to wear seatbelts in cars. In the UK, wearing seatbelts became compulsory in the front seats in 1983 and in the back of the car in 1991.

First published in the United Kingdom in 2014 by
Thames & Hudson Ltd, 181A High Holborn, London WC1V 7QX

Published in association with The National Archives

The National Archives is the UK government's official archive containing over 1,000 years of history. They give detailed guidance to government departments and the public sector on information management, and advise others about the care of historical archives.

www.nationalarchives.gov.uk

British Library Cataloguing-in-Publication Data
A catalogue record for this book is available from the British Library

ISBN 978-0-500-29140-5

Printed and bound in China by Toppan Leefung Printing Limited

To find out about all our publications, please visit **www.thamesandhudson.com**.
There you can subscribe to our e-newsletter, browse or download our current catalogue, and buy any titles that are in print.

PUBLISHER'S NOTE

The caption for each of the detachable posters is given on the reverse side of the image. The name of the designer and the organization that originally published each poster are given where they are known.